Greek

PHRASE BOOK

Compiled by
LEXUS
with
C. Babis Metaxas

HARRAP
London   Paris

Distributed in the United States by
PRENTICE HALL
New York

First published in Great Britain 1989
by HARRAP BOOKS Ltd
Chelsea House, 26 Market Square, Bromley, Kent BR1 1NA

© *Harrap Books Ltd/Lexus Ltd* 1989

ISBN 0 245-54753-3
In the United States, ISBN 0-13-383241-4

Library of Congress Cataloging-in-Publication Data

Harrap's Greek phrase book / compiled by Lexus
with C. Babis Metaxas.
p.   cm.
English and Greek.
"First published in Great Britain, 1989" — T.p. verso.
ISBN 0-13-383241-4 (Prentice Hall)
1. Greek language, Modern — Dictionaries — English.
2. English language — Dictionaries — Greek, Modern.
I. Metaxas, C. Babis. II. Lexus (Firm)
PA1139.E5H37 1990   89-48977
489'.3834'21 — dc20   CIP

Printed and bound in Singapore by
Intellectual Publishing Co.

CONTENTS

THE ALPHABET

A	α	*alfa*	a (as in 'father')
B	β	*vita*	v
Γ	γ	*Gama*	y (as in 'you' or G*)
Δ	δ	*thelta*	th (as in 'the')
E	ε	*epsilon*	e (as in 'red')
Z	ζ	*zita*	z
H	η	*ita*	i (as in 'ski')
Θ	ϑ	*THita*	TH (as in 'theatre')
I	ι	*yota*	i (as in 'ski')
K	κ	*kapa*	k
Λ	λ	*lamtha*	l
M	μ	*mi*	m
N	ν	*ni*	n
Ξ	ξ	*ksi*	x
O	o	*omikron*	o (as in 'hot')
Π	π	*pi*	p
P	ϱ	*ro*	r
Σ	σ, ς**	*siGma*	s
T	τ	*taf*	t
Y	υ	*ipsilon*	i (as in 'ski')
Φ	φ	*fi*	f
X	χ	*chi*	H (as in Scottish 'loch')
Ψ	ψ	*psi*	ps
Ω	ω	*omeGa*	o (as in 'hot')

* see page 6
** this letter is used only at the end of a word

4

The phrase sections in this new book are concise and to the point. In each section you will find: a list of basic vocabulary; a selection of useful phrases; a list of common words and expressions that you will see on signs and notices. A full pronunciation guide is given for things you'll want to say or ask and typical replies to some of your questions are listed.

Of course, there are bound to be occasions when you want to know more. So this book allows for this by containing a two way Greek-English dictionary with a total of some 5,000 references. This will enable you to build up your Greek vocabulary, to make variations on the phrases in the phrase sections and to recognize more of the Greek words that you will see or hear when travelling about.

As well as this we have given a menu reader covering about 200 dishes and types of food — so that you will know what you are ordering! And, as a special feature, there is a section on colloquial Greek.

Speaking the language can make all the difference to your trip. So:

καλή τύχη!
kali tiни!
good luck!

and

καλό ταξίδι!
kalo taksithi!
have a good trip!

PRONUNCIATION

In the phrase sections of this book a pronunciation guide has been given by writing the Greek words as though they were English. So if you read out the pronunciation as English words a Greek should be able to understand you. Also, in the English-Greek dictionary section the translations have been given in a Romanized form so that you can read them directly without reference to the Greek alphabet. Some notes on the pronunciation system:

a	as in 'father'
e	as in 'bed'
g	always hard as in 'girl'
G	a 'g' sound from the back of the throat
H	like the 'ch' in Scottish 'loch'
i	as in 'pitta bread' or 'ski'
o	always short as in 'got'
th	as in 'the' (often close to a 'd')
TH	as in 'theatre'

Letters in bold type in the pronunciation guide mean that this part of the word should be stressed.

Remember that 'e' is always pronounced and never silent. So, for example, the Greek word 'ime' is spoken 'ee-meh' and not to rhyme with 'time'.

In the Greek-English dictionary section we have added a special pronunciation guide at the top of each lefthand page. This gives pronunciation for those characters which are not similar to their Roman alphabet counterparts as well as for some special combinations of letters. The full Greek alphabet is given on page 4.

Note that, in Greek, a semi-colon is used as a question mark.

GENERAL PHRASES

hello
χαίρετε
нercte

hi
γειά
ya

good morning
καλημέρα
kalimera

good evening
καλησπέρα
kalispera

good night
καληνύχτα
kaliniнta

pleased to meet you
χάρηκα
нarika

goodbye
αντίο
adio

cheerio, see you
γειά, θα τα πούμε
ya, тнa ta poome

yes
ναι
ne

no
όχι
oнi

GENERAL PHRASES

yes please
ναι, ευχαριστώ
ne efHaristo

no thank you
όχι, ευχαριστώ
oHi efHaristo

please
σας παρακαλώ
sass parakalo

thank you/thanks
ευχαριστώ
efHaristo

thanks very much
ευχαριστώ πολύ
efHaristo poli

you're welcome
παρακαλώ
parakalo

sorry
συγγνώμη
siGnomi

sorry?/what did you say?
ορίστε;/πώς είπατε;
oriste?; poss ipate?

how are you?
τι κάνετε;/(*familiar*) τι κάνεις;
ti kanete?; ti kaniss?

very well, thank you
πολύ καλά, ευχαριστώ
poli kala efHaristo

and yourself?
εσύ;
essi?

excuse me (*to get attention*)
συγγνώμη
siGnomi

GENERAL PHRASES

how much is it?
πόσο κάνει;
posso kani?

can I ...?
μπορώ να ...;
boro na ...?

can I have ...?
μπορώ να έχω ...;
boro na eho ...?

I'd like to ...
θα ήθελα ...
тна íтнela ...

where is ...?
πού είναι ...;
poo ine ...?

it's not ...
δεν είναι ...
then ine ...

is it ...?
είναι ...;
ine ...?

is there ... here?
υπάρχει ... εδώ;
iparнi ... etho?

could you say that again?
το ξαναλέτε αυτό, σας παρακαλώ;
to ksanalete afto sass parakalo?

please don't speak so fast
λίγο πιο σιγά, σας παρακαλώ
liгo pio siгa sass parakalo

I don't understand
δεν καταλαβαίνω
then katalaveno

OK
εντάξει
endaksi

GENERAL PHRASES

come on, let's go!
άντε, πάμε!
ade pame!

wait for me!
περιμέντε με!
perimende me!

what's your name?
πώς σε λένε;
poss se lene?

what's that in Greek?
πώς το λέμε αυτό στα Ελληνικά;
poss to leme afto sta Elinika?

that's fine!
ωραία!
ore-a!

ανδρών	gents
ανοιχτό	open
απαγορεύεται	forbidden
απαγορεύεται η είσοδος	no entry
απαγορεύεται το κάπνισμα	no smoking
γυναικών	ladies
δεν λειτουργεί	out of order
είσοδος	entrance
ενοικιάζεται	to let
έξοδος	exit
κλειστό	closed
μην πατάτε το πράσινο	keep off the grass
παρακαλώ	please
πληροφορίες	information
πωλείται	for sale
σύρατε	pull
τουαλέτα	toilets
ωθήσατε	push

COMING AND GOING

airport	το αεροδρόμιο	to aerothromio
baggage	οι βαλίτσες	i valitsess
boat	το καράβι	to karavi
book a seat	κλείνω θέση	klino THessi
coach	το πούλμαν	to poolman
docks	η αποβάθρα	i apovaTHra
ferry	το φέρυ-μπωτ	to feri-bot
gate (at airport)	η έξοδος	i eksothoss
harbour	το λιμάνι	to limani
hovercraft	το δελφίνι	to thelfini
plane	το αεροπλάνο	to aeroplano
sleeper	το βαγκόν-λι	to vagon-li
station	ο σταθμός	o staTHmoss
taxi	το ταξί	to taksi
train	το τραίνο	to treno

a ticket to . . .
ένα εισιτήριο για . . .
ena issitirio ya

I'd like to reserve a seat
θα ήθελα να κλείσω μια θέση
THa iTHela na klisso mia THessi

smoking/non-smoking please
καπνίζοντες/μη καπνίζοντες σας παρακαλώ
kapnizondess/mi kapnizondess sass parakalo

a window seat please
μια θέση στο παράθυρο, σας παρακαλώ
mia THessi sto paraTHiro sass parakalo

which platform does the train for . . . leave from?
από ποιά πλατφόρμα φεύγει το τραίνο για . . .,
apo pia platforma fevyi to treno ya?

11

COMING AND GOING

what time is the next flight?
τι ώρα είναι η επόμενη πτήση;
ti ora ine i epomeni ptissi?

is this the right boat for . . .?
αυτό είναι το καράβι για . . .;
afto ine to karavi ya . . .?

is this bus going to . . .?
αυτό το λεωφορείο πάει στην . . .,
afto to leoforio pa-i stin . . .?

is this seat free?
είναι ελεύθερη αυτή η θέση;
ine eleftheri afti i thessi?

do I have to change (buses)?
πρέπει να αλλάξω (λεωφορείο);
prepi na alakso (leoforio)?

is this the right stop for . . .?
αυτή είναι η στάση για . . .;
afti ine i stassi ya . . .?

is this ticket ok?
είναι εντάξει αυτό το εισιτήριο;
ine endaksi afto to issitirio?

I want to change my ticket
θέλω να αλλάξω το εισιτήριο μου
thelo na alakso to issitirio moo

thanks for a lovely stay
σας ευχαριστούμε πολύ, περάσαμε υπέροχα
sass efharistoome poli perassame iperoha

thanks very much for coming to meet me
ευχαριστώ πάρα πολύ μου ήρθατε να με συναντήσετε
efharisto para poli poo irthate na me sinandissete

well, here we are in . . .
λοιπόν, εδώ τώρα είμαστε στο . . .
lipon etho tora imaste sto . . .

COMING AND GOING

ehete tipote na thilossete?
έχετε τίποτε να δηλώσετε;
anything to declare?

*borite na aniksete afti tin tsanda sass
parakalo?*
μπορείτε να ανοίξετε αυτή την
τσάντα, σας παρακαλώ;
would you mind opening this bag please?

Α´ Θέση	first class
αίθουσα αναμονής	waiting room
αλλοδαποί	foreign passports
αναζήτηση αποσκευών	baggage claim
αναχωρήσεις	departures
απαγορεύεται η στάθμευση	no parking
απαγορεύεται το κάπνισμα	no smoking
αφίξεις	arrivals
διόδια	toll
είδη προς δήλωση	something to declare
εισιτήρια	tickets
είσοδος	entrance, way in
έλεγχος διαβατηρίων	passport control
ενοικιάσεις αυτοκινήτων	rent-a-car
έξοδος	exit, way out, gate
καθυστέρηση	delay
κάρτα επιβιβάσεως	boarding pass
καπνίζοντες	smoking (*compartment*)
μη καπνίζοντες	non-smoking (*compartment*)
όριο ταχύτητας	speed limit
ουδέν προς δήλωση	nothing to declare
πληροφορίες	information
προσδεθείτε	fasten your seat belts
τελωνείο	customs
φύλαξη αποσκευών	left luggage
χώρος πάρκινγκ	parking spaces

GETTING A ROOM

balcony	το μπαλκόνι *to balkoni*
bed	το κρεβάτι *to krevati*
breakfast	το πρωινό *to pro-ino*
dinner	το βραδυνό *to vrathino*
dining room	η τραπεζαρία *i trapezaria*
double room	το δίκλινο δωμάτιο *to thiklino thomatio*
guesthouse	η πανσιόν *i panssion*
hotel	το ξενοδοχείο *to ksenothoнio*
key	το κλειδί *to klithi*
lunch	το μεσημεριανό *to messimeriano*
night (*in hotel*)	η βραδυά *i vrathia*
reception	η ρεσεψιόν *i ressepsion*
room	το δωμάτιο *to thomatio*
room with	ένα δωμάτιο με δικό του μπάνιο
private bathroom	*ena thomatio me thiko too banio*
shower	το ντους *to dooz*
single room	το μονόκλινο δωμάτιο *to monoklino thomatio*
with bath	με μπάνιο *me banio*
youth hostel	ο ξενώνας νεότητας *o ksenonass neotitass*

do you have a room for one night?
έχετε ένα δωμάτιο για μια βραδυά;
eнete ena thomatio ya mia vrathya?

do you have a room for one person?
έχετε ένα δωμάτιο για ένα άτομο;
eнete ena thomatio ya ena atomo?

do you have a room for two people?
έχετε ένα δωμάτιο για δύο άτομα;
eнete ena thomatio ya thio atoma?

we'd like to rent a room for a week
θα θέλαμε να νοικιάσουμε ένα δωμάτιο για μια εβδομάδα
тна тнelame na nikiassoome ena thomatio ya mia evthomatha

14

GETTING A ROOM

I'm looking for a good cheap room
ψάχνω για ένα δωμάτιο καλό και φτηνό
psaнno ya ena thomatio kalo ke ftino

I have a reservation
έχω κλείσει δωμάτιο
eнo klissi thomatio

how much is it?
πόσο κάνει;
posso kani?

can I see the room please?
μπορώ να δω το δωμάτιο, σας παρακαλώ;
boro na tho to thomatio sass parakalo?

does that include breakfast?
είναι το πρωινό μέσα στην τιμή;
ine to pro-ino messa stin timi?

a room overlooking the sea
ένα δωμάτιο με θέα στην θάλασσα
ena thomatio me тнe-a stin тнalassa

we'd like to stay another night
θα θέλαμε να μείνουμε άλλη μια βραδυά
тнa тнelame na minoome ali mia vrathya

we will be arriving late *(at a late hour)*
θα φτάσουμε αργά
тнa ftassoome arгa

(later than we said)
θα φτάσουμε πιο αργά από ότι είχαμε πει
тнa ftassoome pio arгa apo oti iнame pi

can I have my bill please?
τον λογαριασμό, σας παρακαλώ
ton loгariasmo sass parakalo

I'll pay cash
θα πληρώσω τοις μετρητοίς
тнa plirosso tiss metritiss

GETTING A ROOM

can I pay by credit card?
μπορώ να πληρώσω με κάρτα;
boro na plirosso me karta?

will you give me a call at 6.30 in the morning?
μπορείτε να με ξυπνήσετε στις έξι και μισή το πρωί;
borite na me ksipnissete stiss eksi ke missi to pro-i?

at what time do you serve breakfast/dinner?
τι ώρα είναι το πρωινό/το βραδυνό;
ti ora ine to pro-ino/to vrathino?

can we have breakfast in our room?
μπορείτε να μας φέρετε το πρωινό στο δωμάτιο;
borite na mass ferete to pro-ino sto thomatio?

thanks for putting us up
ευχαριστούμε για την φιλοξενία
efnaristoome ya tin filoksenia

Ι^{ος} όροφος	first floor
Α΄ κατηγορίας	first class (*hotel*)
ανδρών	gentlemen
ανελκυστήρας	lift
γυναικών	ladies
ενοικιάζονται δωμάτια	rooms to rent
έξοδος κινδύνου	emergency exit
εστιατόριο	restaurant
ισόγειο	ground floor
μην ενοχλείτε	do not disturb
μπάνιο	bathroom
μπαρ	bar
ντουζ	shower
ξενοδοχείο	hotel
ξενώνας νεότητας	youth hostel
πρωινό	breakfast
πυροσβεστήρας	fire extinguisher
σύρατε	pull
τραπεζαρία	dining room
υπόγειο	basement
ωθήσατε	push

bill	ο λογαριασμός	o loɢariasmoss
dessert	το γλυκό	to ɢliko
drink	πίνω	pino
eat	τρώω	tro-o
food	το φαγητό	to fa-yito
main course	το κυρίως πιάτο	to kirioss piato
menu	ο κατάλογος	o kataloɢoss
restaurant	το εστιατόριο	to estiatorio
salad	η σαλάτα	i salata
starter	το πρώτο πιάτο	to proto piato
tip	το φιλοδώρημα	to filothorima
waiter	το γκαρσόν	to garson

a table for three, please
ένα τραπέζι για τρεις, σας παρακαλώ
ena trapezi ya triss sass parakalo

can I see the menu?
μπορώ να δω τον κατάλογο;
boro na tho ton kataloɢo?

we'd like to order
μπορούμε να παραγγείλουμε;
boroome na paragiloome

what do you recommend?
εσείς, τι θα μας προτείνατε;
essiss ti тна mass protinate?

I'd like . . . please
θα ήθελα . . . σας παρακαλώ
тна ітнеla . . . sass parakalo

waiter!
γκαρσόν!
garson!

EATING OUT

waitress!
δεσποινίς!
thespiniss!

could we have the bill, please?
τον λογαριασμό, σας παρακαλώ
ton locariasmo sass parakalo

two white coffees please
δυό καφέδες με γάλα, σας παρακαλώ
thio kafethess me cala sass parakalo

that's for me
αυτό είναι για μένα
afto ine ya mena

some more bread please
λίγο ψωμί ακόμη, σας παρακαλώ
lico psomi akomi sass parakalo

a bottle of red/white wine please
ένα μπουκάλι κόκκινο/άσπρο κρασί, σας
παρακαλώ
ena bookali kokino/aspro krassi sass parakalo

εστιατόριο	restaurant
ζαχαροπλαστείο	café, patisserie
καφετερία	café
μεζέδες	appetizers
ουζερί	ouzo bar
ποικιλία	a selection of appetizers
ταβέρνα	informal restaurant (*originally a drinking place*)
της ώρας	dishes grilled/fried to order
ψαροταβέρνα	fish restaurant
ψησταριά	restaurant specialising in charcoal-grilled/roasted meat

Ways of cooking, sauces etc

αυγολέμονο avɢolemono *egg and lemon sauce*
βραστό vrasto *boiled*
γεμιστά yemista *stuffed, usually with rice and/or minced meat*
καπνιστό kapnisto *smoked*
κοκκινιστό kokinisto *in tomato sauce*
κρασάτο krassato *cooked in wine sauce*
λαδερά lathera *in olive oil and tomato sauce*
με λαδολέμονο me latholemono *with olive oil and lemon dressing*
με σάλτσα me saltsa *with sauce, usually tomato sauce*
παστό pasto *salted*
πλακί plaki *baked in the oven in a tomato sauce*
στο φούρνο sto foorno *baked in the oven*
σωτέ sote *lightly fried*
τηγανητό tiɢanito *fried*
της κατσαρόλας tiss katsarolass *casseroled*
της σούβλας tiss soovlass *roast on a spit*
της σχάρας tiss sнarass *grilled over charcoal*
τουρσί toorsi *pickled*
ψητό psito *grilled over charcoal; oven-roasted*

Common food items

αγγουράκια agoorakyia *cucumbers*
αμύγδαλα amiɢthala *almonds*
αρακάς arakass *peas*
αρνάκι arnaki *lamb*
αρνί arni *mutton*
αστακός astakoss *lobster*
αχλάδια aнlathia *pears*

βερύκοκα verikoka *apricots*
βωδινό vothino *beef*

γαλοπούλα ɢalopoola *turkey*

19

MENU READER

γαρίδες Garithess *prawns*
γλῶσσα ylossa *tongue; sole*

ελαιόλαδο eleolatho *olive oil*
ελιές eli-ess *olives*

θαλασσινά THalassina *seafood*

καλαμαράκια kalamarakia *squid*
καραβίδες karavithess *king prawns*
καρπούζι karpoozi *watermelon*
κασέρι kasseri *Cheddar-type cheese*
κεράσια kerassia *cherries*
κεφαλοτύρι kefalotiri *type of cheese*
κολοκυθάκια kolokiTHakia *courgettes*
κότα kota *chicken*
κοτόπουλο kotopoolo *chicken*
κουνέλι kooneli *rabbit*
κουνουπίδι koonoopithi *cauliflower*
κρέας kreass *meat, usually beef*
κρεμμυδάκια kremithakia *spring onions*
κρεμμύδια kremithia *onions*

λαζάνια lazania *tagliatelle*
λαχανικά laHanika *vegetables*
λάχανο laHano *cabbage*
λιθρίνι liTHrini *red snapper (fish)*

μαϊντανός maidanoss *parsley*
μακαρόνια makaronia *pasta*
μανιτάρια manitaria *mushrooms*
μανταρίνια mandarinia *tangerines*
μέλι meli *honey*
μελιτζάνες melidzaness *aubergines*
μήλα mila *apples*
μοσχάρι mosHari *veal; tender beef*
μπακαλιάρος bakaliaros *cod, salt cod*
μπάμιες bami-ess *okra*
μπαρμπούνια barboonia *red mullet*
μπριζόλες brizoless *chops, steaks*
μυαλά miala *brains*
μύδια mithia *mussels*

ντομάτες domatess *tomatoes*

ξηροί καρποί ksiri karpi *nuts, dried fruit*

20

ξιφίας ksifiass *swordfish*
παγωτό paɢoto *ice cream*
παντζάρι pandzari *beetroot*
πατάτες patatess *potatoes*
πατσάς patsass *tripe*
πεπόνι peponi *melon*
πέστροφα pestrofa *trout*
πιλάφι pilafi *rice*
πιπέρι piperi *pepper (spice)*
πιπεριά piperia *pepper (vegetable)*
πορτοκάλι portokali *orange*
πράσο prasso *leek*

ρίγανη riɢani *oregano*
ροδάκινα rothakina *peaches*

σαρδέλλες sartheless *sardines*
σέλινο selino *celery*
σκόρδο skortho *garlic*
σουπιές soopi-ess *cuttlefish*
σταφίδες stafithess *currants; sultanas*
σταφύλια stafilia *grapes*
στρείδια strithia *oysters*
σύκα sika *figs*

ταραμάς taramass *cod roe*
τόννος tonnoss *tuna*
τσιπούρα tsipoora *sea bream*
τυρί tiri *cheese*

φάβα fava *split peas*
φασολάκια fassolakia *green beans*
φασόλια fassolia *beans*
φέτα feta *feta cheese*
φιλέτο fileto *fillet*
φράουλες fra-ooless *strawberries*
φρούτα froota *fruit*
φυστίκια fistikia *peanuts*
φυστίκια Αιγίνης fistikia Eyiniss *pistachios*

χοιρινό ɧirino *pork*
χταπόδι ɧtaqothi *octopus*

ψάρια psaria *fish*

MENU READER

Some typical dishes

αρνάκι εξοχικό arnaki eksoнiko *leg of lamb baked in greaseproof paper*

αρνάκι με μπάμιες arnaki me bami-ess *lamb and okra stew*

αρνάκι με πατάτες στο φούρνο arnaki me patatess sto foorno *roast lamb and potatoes*

αρνάκι τας κεμπάπ arnaki tass kebap *lamb in tomato sauce*

αρνάκι της σούβλας arnaki tiss soovlass *lamb roast on the spit*

αρνάκι φρικασέ με μαρούλια arnaki frikasse me maroolia *lamb and lettuce in an egg and lemon sauce*

αυγά μάτια avga matia *fried eggs*

αυγά μελάτα avga melata *soft-boiled eggs*

αυγά σφιχτά avga sfiнta *hard-boiled eggs*

βωδινό βραστό vothino vrasto *borscht-like beef stew*

γαλακτομπούρεκο galaktobooreko *cream-filled sweet 'filo' pastry*

γαρδούμπα garthooba *rolled lamb offal on a spit*

γιουβαρλάκια αυγολέμονο yoovarlakia avgolemono *meatballs with rice in egg and lemon sauce*

γιουβέτσι yoovetsi *lamb with a kind of pasta*

γλυκό βύσσινο gliko vissino *candied cherries in syrup*

γλυκό σύκο gliko siko *candied figs in syrup*

καλαμαράκια τηγανητά kalamarakia tiganita *fried squid*

κανταΐφι kada-ifi *shredded and rolled 'filo' pastry in syrup*

καρυδόπιττα karithopita *walnut cake*

κεφτέδες keftethess *meatballs*

κοκορέτσι kokoretsi *rolled lamb offal on a spit*

κολοκυθάκια γιαχνί kolokiтнakia yaнni *courgettes and onions in a tomato sauce*

κολοκυθάκια με κρέας kolokiтнakia me kreass *courgettes and beef stew* κοτόπουλο κοκκινιστό kotopoolo kokinisto *chicken in tomato soup*

κοτόπουλο της σούβλας kotopoolo tiss soovlass *chicken roast on the spit*

κρεατόπιττα kreatopita *minced meat in 'filo' pastry*

λαγός στιφάδο laGoss stifatho *hare and shallot stew*

λαχανοντολμάδες laHanodolmathess *cabbage leaves stuffed with minced meat and rice*

λουκουμάδες lookoomathess *fried doughnuts in syrup*

λουκούμια lookoomia *Turkish delight*

μακαρόνια με κιμά makaronia me kima *spaghetti bolognaise*

μακαρόνια παστίτσιο makaronia pastitsio *layers of pasta and mince/cheese topped with bechamel*

μελιτζάνες μουσακά melidzaness moossaka *layers of aubergine and mince topped with bechamel*

μελιτζάνες παπουτσάκια melidzaness papootsakia *stuffed aubergines*

μελιτζανοσαλάτα melidzanosalata *puréed aubergine salad*

μοσχάρι με μελιτζάνες mosHari me melidzaness *veal and aubergine stew*

μοσχάρι με φασολάκια mosHari me fassolakia *veal and green beans*

μοσχάρι ψητό mosHari psito *pot-roast veal*

μουσακάς moossakass *moussaka (layers of vegetables and minced meat topped with bechamel sauce)*

μπακλαβάς baklavass *baklava ('filo' pastry with nuts and syrup)*

μπάμιες λαδερές bami-ess latheress *okra in olive oil and tomato sauce*

μπιφτέκι bifteki *hamburger*

μπουγάτσα booGatsa *puff pastry with various fillings*

μπριάμι briami *ratatouille*

μπριζόλες χοιρινές στη σχάρα brizoless Hiriness sti sHara *pork chops grilled over charcoal* ντολμάδες **dolmathess** *vine or cabbage leaves stuffed with minced meat and/or rice*

ντομάτες γεμιστές **domatess yemistess** *stuffed tomatoes*

πατάτες γιαχνί **patatess yahni** *potatoes and onions in tomato sauce*

πατάτες πιγανάτες στο φούρνο **patatess riganatess sto foorno** *oven-cooked potatoes with oregano*

πιπεριές γεμιστές **piperi-ess yemistess** *stuffed green peppers*

ρυζόγαλο **rizogalo** *rice pudding*

σκορδαλιά **skorthalia** *thick garlic sauce*

σουβλάκια **soovlakia** *meat off a skewer, served in pitta bread*

σουπιές με σπανάκι **soopi-ess me spanaki** *cuttlefish and spinach stew*

στιφάδο **stifatho** *chopped meat with onions*

συκώτι ψητό **sikoti psito** *liver grilled over charcoal*

τζατζίκι **dzadziki** *yogurt and cucumber dip*

τσουρέκι **tsooreki** *light sponge*

τυρόπιττα **tiropita** *cheese and egg in 'filo' pastry*

φακές **fakess** *lentil soup*

φασολάδα **fassolatha** *bean soup with celery, carrots and tomatoes*

φασολάκια λαδερά **fassolakia lathera** *green beans in olive oil and tomato sauce*

φασόλια γίγαντες **fassolia yigandess** *large dried beans in tomato sauce*

χαλβάς **halvass** *sweet made from sesame seeds, nuts and honey*

χταποδάκι ξυδάτο **htapothaki ksithato** *pickled octopus*

χωριάτικη σαλάτα **horiatiki salata** *tomatoes, cucumber, cheese, peppers, olives and boiled eggs with olive oil and vinegar dressing*

ψαρόσουπα **psarossoopa** *fish soup*

HAVING A DRINK

bar	το μπαρ *to bar*
beer	η μπύρα *i bira*
coke (R)	η κόκα-κόλα *i koka-kola*
dry	ξερό *ksero*
fresh orange	το πορτοκάλι χυμός *to portokali himoss*
gin and tonic	το τζιν με τόνικ *to gin me tonik*
ice	ο πάγος *o pagoss*
lager	η μπύρα *i bira*
lemonade	η λεμονάδα *i lemonatha*
red	κόκκινό *kokino*
straight (*no ice*)	χωρίς πάγο. *horiss pago*
(*no mixers*)	σκέτο *sketo*
sweet	γλυκό *gliko*
vodka	η βότκα *i votka*
whisky	το ουίσκυ *to wiski*
white	άσπρο *aspro*
wine	το κρασί *to krassi*

let's go for a drink
πάμε για ένα ποτό
pame ya ena poto

a beer please
μιά μπύρα, σας παρακαλώ
mia bira sass parakalo

two beers please
δύο μπύρες, σας παρακαλώ
thio biress sass parakalo

a glass of red/white wine
ένα ποτήρι κόκκινο/άσπρο κρασί
ena potiri kokino/aspro krassi

with lots of ice
με πολύ πάγο
me poli pago

HAVING A DRINK

no ice thanks
χωρίς πάγο, σας παρακαλώ
ноriss paго sass parakalo

can I have another one?
ακόμη ένα;
akomi ena?

the same again please
το ίδιο πάλι, σας παρακαλώ
to ithio pali sass parakalo

what'll you have?
τι θα πιείτε; *(familiar)* τι θα πιείς;
ti тна p-yite?; ti тна p-yiss?

I'll get this round
τώρα, κερνάω εγώ
tora kernao eгo

not for me thanks
εγώ δεν θέλω τίποτε, ευχαριστώ
eгo then тнelo tipote efнaristo

he's absolutely smashed
αυτός είναι τύφλα στο μεθύσι
aftos ine tifla sto meтнissi

άσπρο/κόκκινο κρασί *aspro/kokino krassi* white/red
   wine
ελληνικός καφές *elinikoss kafess* Greek coffee

σκέτος *sketoss* 1 teaspoonful coffee – no sugar
με ολίγη *me oliгi* 1 teaspoonful coffee, half
   teaspoonful sugar
μέτριος *metrioss* 1 tsp coffee, 1 tsp sugar
βαρύγλυκος *variclikoss* 1 tsp coffee, 2 tsp sugar
γαλλικός καφές *гalikoss kafess* filter coffee
νέσκαφε *neskafe* instant coffee
νέσκαφε φραπέ *neskafe frape* ice cold instant coffee
μεταλλικό νερό *metaliko nero* mineral water
ούζο *oozo* ouzo

26

COLLOQUIAL EXPRESSIONS

barmy	ψώνιο *pssonio*
bird	η γκόμενα *i gomena*
bloke	ο τύπος *o tiposs*
nutter	θεότρελλος *THeotreloss*
pissed	πίττα *pita*
thickie	βλάκας *vlakass*
twit	ανόητος *ano-itoss*

great!
άψογο!
apsoco!

that's awful!
απαίσιο!
apessio!

shut up!
σκασμός!
skasmoss!

ouch!
ωχ!
oH!

yum-yum!
μούρλια!
moorlia!

I'm absolutely knackered
είμαι πτώμα στην κούραση
ime ptoma stin koorassi

I'm fed up
βαριέμαι που ζω
varyeme poo zo

I'm fed up with ...
έχω βαρεθεί με ...
eHo vareTHi me ...

COLLOQUIAL EXPRESSIONS

don't make me laugh!
έλα, άσε τα αστεία!
ela asse ta astia!

you've got to be joking!
πλάκα κάνεις, σίγουρα!
plaka kanis siGoora!

it's rubbish (goods etc)
για πέταμα είναι
ya petama ine

it's a rip-off
φοβερή κλεψιά
foveri klepsia

get lost!
φύγε αμέσως!
fiye amessoss!

it's a damn nuisance
μεγάλος μπελάς
meGaloss belass

it's absolutely fantastic
φοβερό, καταπληκτικό, απίθανο!
fovero katapliktiko apíтнano!

άντε!	*ade!* come on!
αυτός είσαι!	*aftoss isse!* that's my boy!
έγινε!	*eyine!* OK, coming up
μάγκας	*maĸass* streetwise person
μαλάκας	*malakass* idiot
πρώτα!	*prota* great!
ρε συ!	*re si!* you, there!
χάλια!	*нalia!* awful!

28

bike	το ποδήλατο *to pothilato*
boat	το καράβι *to karavi*
bus	το λεωφορείο *to leoforio*
car	το αυτοκίνητο *to aftokinito*
change (*buses*)	αλλάζω *alazo*
ferry	το φέρυ-μπωτ *to feri-bot*
garage (*for fuel*)	το βενζινάδικο *to venzinathiko*
hitch-hiking	το ώτο-στοπ *to oto-stop*
hydrofoil	το δελφίνι *to thelfini*
map	ο χάρτης *o нartiss*
moped	το μηχανάκι *to miнanaki*
motorbike	η μοτοσυκλέτα *i motossikleta*
petrol	η βενζίνη *i venzini*
return (*ticket*)	(εισιτήριο) με επιστροφή (*issitirio*) *me epistrofi*
single	μόνο να πάω *mono na pao*
station	ο σταθμός *o statнmoss*
taxi	το ταξί *to taksi*
ticket	το εισιτήριο *to issitirio*
train	το τραίνο *to treno*

I'd like to rent a car/bike/moped
θα ήθελα να νοικιάσω ένα αυτοκίνητο/ποδήλατο/
μηχανάκι
тна íтнela na nikiasso ena aftokinito/pothilato/miнanaki

how much is it per day?
πόσο πάει τη μέρα;
posso pa-i ti mera?

when do I have to bring the car back?
πότε πρέπει να το επιστρέψω το αυτοκίνητο;
pote prepi na to epistrepso to aftokinito?

I'm heading for ...
πάω για ...
pao ya ...

29

GETTING AROUND

how do I get to . . .?
πώς θα πάω στο . . .;
poss THA pao sto . . .?

REPLIES

issia, efrHia
ίσια, ευθεία
straight on

stripsse aristera/theksia
στρίψε αριστερά/δεξιά
turn left/right

ine afto eki to ktirio
είναι αυτό εκεί το κτίριο
it's that building there

ine pross ta pisso
είναι προς τα πίσω
it's back that way

proto/theftero/trito aristera
πρώτο/δεύτερο/τρίτο αριστερά
first/second/third on the left

we're just travelling around
έτσι, γυρνάμε, όπου μας βγάλει
etsi, yirname, opoo mass vgali

I'm a stranger here
ξένος είμαι
ksenoss ime

is that on the way?
είναι στον δρόμο μας;
ine ston thromo mass?

can I get off here?
μπορώ να κατεβώ εδώ;
boro na katevo etho?

two returns to . . . please
δύο εισιτήρια με επιστροφή για . . . σας παρακαλώ
thio issitiria me epistrofi ya . . . sass parakalo

GETTING AROUND

what time is the last bus back?
τι ώρα είναι το τελευταίο λεωφορείο για πίσω;
ti ora ine to telefteo leoforio ya pisso

we want to leave tomorrow and come back the day after
θέλουμε να φύγουμε αύριο και να γυρίσουμε μεθαύριο
THeloome na fiyoome avrio ke na yirissoome meTHavrio

we're coming back the same day
θα γυρίσουμε την ίδια μέρα
THa yirissoome tin ithia mera

is this the right stop for ...?
αυτή είναι η στάση για ...;
afti ine i stassi ya ...?

is this bus going to ...?
πάει αυτο το λεωφορείο στο ...;
pa-i,afto to leoforio sto ...?

which village is this?
ποιό χωριό είναι αυτό;
pio Horio ine afto?

which stop is it for ...?
ποιά στάση είναι για ...;
pia stassi ine ya ...?

can I take my bike on the bus?
μπορώ να πάρω το ποδήλατο μου στο λεωφορείο;
boro na paro to pothilato moo sto leoforio?

how far is it to the nearest petrol station?
πόσο μακριά είναι για το πιο κοντινό βενζινάδικο;
posso makria ine ya to pio kondino venzinathiko?

I need a new tyre
θέλω καινούργιο λάστιχο
THelo kenooryio lastiHo

it's overheating
έχει ζεσταθεί πολύ η μηχανή
eHi zestatHi poli i miHani

GETTING AROUND

there's something wrong with the brakes
κάποιο πρόβλημα υπάρχει με τα φρένα
kapio provlima iparнi me ta frena

απαγορεύεται η είσοδος	no entry
απαγορεύεται η στάθμευση	no parking
απαγορεύεται η στάση	no waiting
απαγορεύεται η στροφή δεξιά/αριστερά	no right/left turn
απλή	2 star petrol
αφετηρία	departure point (*buses*)
δακτύλιος	inner city restricted zone (*cars with even/odd numbers on licence plates banned on alternate days*)
διάβαση πεζών	pedestrian crossing
διόδια	toll
εισιτήρια	tickets
ελεύθερο	for hire (*taxi*)
εκτελούνται έργα	roadworks ahead
ενοικιάσεις αυτοκινήτων	car rental
ηλεκτρικός	underground
κίνδυνος!	danger!
μονόδρομος	one way street
όριο ταχύτητας	speed limit
παρακαμπτήριος	diversion
προσοχή!	attention!
προτεραιότητα δεξιά	vehicles coming from the right have priority
σούπερ	4 star petrol
σταθμός ηλεκτρικού	underground station
στάση	bus stop
στάση ταξί	taxi rank
τέρμα	destination (*buses*)
τροχαία	traffic police
χώρος πάρκινγκ	parking spaces

SHOPPING

carrier bag	η τσάντα *i tsanda*
(*plastic*)	η σακούλα *i sakoola*
cashdesk	το ταμείο *to tamio*
cheap	φτηνό *ftino*
cheque	η επιταγή *i epita-yi*
department	το τμήμα *to tmima*
expensive	ακριβό *akrivo*
pay	πληρώνω *plirono*
receipt	η απόδειξη *i apothiksi*
shop	το μαγαζί *to macazi*
shop assistant	(*male*) ο υπάλληλος *o ipaliloss*
	(*female*) η πωλήτρια *i politria*
supermarket	το σουπερμάρκετ *to soopermarket*
till	το ταμείο *to tamio*

I'd like . . .
θα ήθελα . . .
THa íтНela . . .

have you got . . .?
έχετε . . .;
eHete . . .

can I just have a look around?
μπορώ να ρίξω μια ματιά;
boro na rikso mia matia?

that's too much
είναι πολύ ακριβό
ine poli akrivo

how much is this?
πόσο κάνει αυτό;
posso kani afto?

the one in the window
αυτό στην βιτρίνα
afto stin vitrina

SHOPPING

do you take credit cards ?
δέχεστε πιστωτικές κάρτες;
theнeste pistotikess kartess?

I'd like to try it on
θα ήθελα να το δοκιμάσω
тнa ітнela na to thokimasso

I'll come back
θα ξανάρθω
тнa ksanarтнo

it's too big/small
είναι πολύ μεγάλο/μικρό
ine poli meсalo/mikro

it's not what I'm looking for
δεν είναι αυτό που θέλω
then ine afto poo тнelo

I'll take it
θα το πάρω
тнa to paro

can you gift-wrap it?
μπορείτε να το τυλίξετε για δώρο;
borite na to tiliksete ya thoro?

ανοιχτό	open
καπνοπωλείο – ψιλικά	tobacco and sundry small items
εκπτώσεις	sale
κατανάλωση πριν από . . .	consume before . . .
κλειστό	closed
ταμείο	cash point
τρόφιμα – ποτά	food – drinks
φυλάσσεται σε μέρος δροσερό	keep in a cool place
ώρες λειτουργίας	opening hours

Αγιο Ορος (το)	Mount Athos, a monastic state in the Halkidiki peninsula
αρχαία (τα)	the ancient Greek language; an archaeological site
Δωδεκάνησα (τα)	the 'twelve islands' (Rhodes, Kos etc) in the SE Aegean
Εμφύλιος (ο)	the Greek Civil War 1946-1949
Επτάνησα (τα)	the 'seven islands' (Corfu, Ithaca etc) in the Ionian Sea
ζέμπέκικο (το)	a solo man's dance to 'rebetika' music
Ιόνιο (το)	the Ionian Sea
Κυκλάδες (οι)	the Cycladic islands (Mykonos, Santorini etc)
Μακεδονία (η)	Macedonia; Northern Greece
Μεγάλη Εβδομάδα (η)	Holy Week
Μικρασιάτες (οι)	Greeks from Asia Minor
Παρθενώνας (ο)	the Parthenon
Πάσχα (το)	Easter Sunday
Πόντιοι (οι)	Greeks from the coast of the Black Sea
ρεμπέτικα (τα)	Greek urban folk songs
Ρωμιοσύνη (η)	the Greek nation; Greek national character
25 Μαρτίου	25th March 1821, Independence Day
Σποράδες (οι)	the islands of the NW Aegean (Skiathos etc)
τσιφτετέλι (το)	the Greek version of belly-dancing
φιλότιμο (το)	pride; keenness to prove oneself
χασάπικο (το)	a mixed group dance to 'rebetika' music
χούντα (η)	the Colonels' regime 1967-1974

MONEY

bank	η τράπεζα *i trapeza*
bill	ο λογαριασμός *o loɕariasmoss*
bureau de change	το γραφείο συναλλάγματος *to ɕrafio sinalaɕmatoss*
change (*small*)	τα ψιλά *ta psila*
cheque	η επιταγή *i epita-yi*
credit card	η πιστωτική κάρτα *i pistotiki karta*
drachmas	οι δραχμές *i thraнmess*
exchange rate	η νομισματική ισοτιμία *i nomismatiki isotimia*
expensive	ακριβό *akrivo*
pounds (sterling)	οι λίρες στερλίνες *i liress sterliness*
price	η τιμή *i timi*
receipt	η απόδειξη *i apothiksi*
traveller's cheque	ταξιδιωτική επιταγή *i taksithyotiki epita-yi*

how much is it?
πόσο κάνει;
posso kani?

I'd like to change this into . . .
θα ήθελα να το αλλάξω αυτό σε . . .
тнa íтнela na to alakso afto se . . .

can you give me something smaller?
μπορείτε να μου δώσετε ψιλά;
borite na moo thossete psila?

can I use this credit card?
δέχονται αυτήν εδώ την κάρτα;
тненonde aftin etho tin karta?

can we have the bill please?
τον λογαριασμό, σας παρακαλώ
ton loɕariasmo sass parakalo

36

MONEY

please keep the change
κρατήστε τα ρέστα
kratiste ta resta

does that include service?
είναι και το φιλοδώρημα μέσα;
ine ke to filothorima messa?

I think the figures are wrong
νομίζω ότι υπάρχει κάποιο λάθος
nomizo oti iparнi kapio laтноss

I don't have any money
δεν έχω καθόλου λεφτά
then eнo катноloo lefta

The unit is the drachma δραχμή (*dhraн-mi*) often
abbreviated to δρχ, and, colloquially, often referred
to as: το φράγκο (*fran-go*). Colloquially, various coins
and notes are known as

2 δρχ	το δίφραγκο	*thifrago*
5 δρχ	το τάληρο	*taliro*
10 δρχ	το δεκάρικο	*thekariko*
20 δρχ	το εικοσάρικο	*ikossariko*
50 δρχ	το πενηντάρικο	*penidariko*
100 δρχ	το κατοστάρικο	*to katostariko*
500 δρχ	το πεντακοσάρικο	*to pedakossariko*
1000 δρχ	το χιλιάρικο	*to нiliariko*
5000 δρχ	το πεντοχίλιαρο	*to pedoнiliaro*

δολλάριο	United States dollar
λίρα Αγγλίας	pound sterling
συνάλλαγμα	foreign exchange
ταμείο	cash point; teller
τιμές συναλλάγματος: αγορά . . .	exchange rate: we buy . . .
τιμές συναλλάγματος: πώληση . . .	exchange rate: we sell . . .
τράπεζα	bank

ENTERTAINMENT

band (*pop*)	το συγκρότημα *to sigrotima*
cinema	το σινεμά *to sinema*
concert	το κοντσέρτο *to kontserto*
disco	η ντισκοτέκ *i diskotek*
film	το φιλμ *to film*
go out	βγαίνω *vyeno*
music	η μουσική *i moosiki*
play (*theatre*)	το θεατρικό έργο *to theatriko ergo*
seat	η θέση *i thessi*
show	η παράσταση *i parastassi*
singer	(*male*) ο τραγουδιστής *o tra-yoothistis*
	(*female*) η τραγουδίστρια *i tra-yoothistria*
theatre	το θέατρο *to theatro*
ticket	το εισιτήριο *to issitirio*

are you doing anything tonight?
έχεις να κάνεις τίποτε απόψε;
ehiss na kaniss tipote apopse?

do you want to come out with me tonight?
θέλεις να βγούμε απόψε;
theliss na vyoome apopse?

what's on?
πού έχει να πάμε;
poo ehi na pame?

have you got a programme of what's on in town?
έχετε κανένα οδηγό θεαμάτων;
ehete kanena othigo theamaton?

(in Athens) έχετε το "Αθηνόραμα";
ehete to "Athinorama"?

which is the best disco round here?
ποιά είναι η πιο καλή ντισκοτέκ εδώ κοντά;
pia ine i pio kali diskotek etho konda?

38

ENTERTAINMENT

let's go to the cinema/theatre
πάμε σινεμά/στο θέατρο
pame sinema/sto theatro

I've seen it
το έχω δει
to eho thi

I'll meet you at 9 o'clock outside the cinema
θα βρεθούμε στις εννιά έξω από το σινεμά
tha vrethoome stis enia ekso apo to sinema

can I have two tickets for tonight?
θα ήθελα δύο εισιτήρια για απόψε
tha ithela thio issitiria ya apopse

do you want to dance (again)?
θέλεις να χορέψουμε (πάλι);
theliss na horepssoome (pali)?

thanks but I'm with my boyfriend
ευχαριστώ πολύ, αλλά είμαι με τον φίλο μου
efharisto poli ala ime me ton filo moo

let's go out for some fresh air
ας βγούμε να πάρουμε λίγο αέρα
ass vyoome na paroome ligo a-era

will you let me back in again later?
θα με αφήσετε να ξαναμπώ;
tha me afissete na ksanabo?

I'm meeting someone inside
έχω ραντεβού με κάποιον μέσα
eho randevoo me kapion messa

ακατάλληλο	18 and over only
διάλειμμα	interval
εισιτήρια	tickets
κατάλληλο	U-certificate
κλειστό	closed
μπουζούκια	place for live Greek music

THE BEACH

beach	η παραλία *i paralia*
beach umbrella	η ομπρέλλα της πλαζ *i obrela tiss plaz*
bikini	το μπικίνι *to bikini*
dive	κάνω βουτιά *kano vootia*
sand	η άμμος *i amoss*
sea	η θάλασσα *i thalassa*
sunbathe	κάνω ηλιοθεραπεία *kano iliotherapia*
suntan lotion	αντιηλιακή λοσιόν *andi-iliaki lossion*
suntan oil	αντιηλιακό λάδι *andi-iliako lathi*
swim	κολυμπάω *kolibao*
swimming costume	το μαγιό *to mayo*
tan (*verb*)	μαυρίζω *mavrizo*
towel	η πετσέτα *i petseta*
wave	το κύμα *to kima*

let's go down to the beach
πάμε στην παραλία
pame stin paralia

what's the water like?
πώς είναι το νερό;
poss ine to nero?

it's freezing
είναι παγωμένο
ine pagomeno

it's beautiful
είναι υπέροχο
ine iperoho

are you coming for a swim?
θα έρθεις για μπάνιο;
tha erthiss ya banio?

I can't swim
δεν ξέρω να κολυμπάω
then ksero na kolibao

THE BEACH

he swims like a fish
κολυμπάει σαν δελφίνι
koliba-i san thelfini

will you keep an eye on my things for me?
μπορείς να προσέχεις τα πράγματα μου;
boriss na prossehiss ta pragmata moo?

is it deep here?
είναι βαθειά εδώ;
ine vathia etho?

could you rub suntan oil on my back?
μπορείς να μου βάλεις λάδι στην πλάτη;
boriss na moo valiss lathi stin plati?

I love sun bathing
μου αρέσει πάρα πολύ η ηλιοθεραπεία
moo aressi para poli i iliotherapia

I'm all sunburnt
έχω καεί ολόκληρος από τον ήλιο
eho ka-i oklokliross apo ton ilio

you're all wet!
είσαι μούσκεμα!
isse mooskema!

let's go up to the cafe
πάμε πάνω στο καφενείο
pame pano sto kafenio

απαγορεύεται ο γυμνισμός	nudism is prohibited
αχινός	sea urchin
ενοικιάζονται βάρκες	boats for hire
καμπίνες	changing rooms
μολυσμένα ύδατα	polluted water
ντους	showers
παραλία	beach
τσούχτρα	jellyfish

41

accident	το ατύχημα *to atiнima*
ambulance	το ασθενοφόρο *to astнenoforo*
broken	σπασμένο *spasmeno*
doctor	ο γιατρός *o yatross*
fire	η φωτιά *i fotia*
fire brigade	η πυροσβεστική *i pirosvestiki*
ill	άρρωστος *arostoss*
injured	τραυματίας *travmatiass*
late	αργά *arga*
police	η αστυνομία *i asstinomia*

can you help me? I'm lost
μπορείτε να με βοηθήσετε; έχω χαθεί
borite na me vo-itнissete, eнo натнi

I've lost my passport
έχω χάσει το διαβατήριο μου
eнo нassi to thiavatirio moo

I've locked myself out of my room
κλειδώθηκα απέξω από το δωμάτιο μου
klithoтнika apekso apo to thomatio moo

my luggage hasn't arrived
δεν έχουν έρθει οι βαλίτσες μου
then eнoon ertнi i valitsess moo

I can't get it open
δεν μπορώ να το ανοίξω
then boro na to anikso

it's jammed
έχει φρακάρει
eнi frakari

I don't have enough money
δεν έχω αρκετά λεφτά
then eнo arketa lefta

42

PROBLEMS

I've broken down
χάλασε το αυτοκίνητο
Halasse to aftokinito

this is an emergency
είναι επείγον
ine epiGon

help!
βοήθεια!
voîtHia!

it doesn't work, it's out of order
δεν δουλεύει
then thoolevi

the lights aren't working in my room
δεν έχει φως στο δωμάτιο μου
then eHi foss sto thomatio moo

the lift is stuck
σταμάτησε το ασανσέρ
stamatisse to assansser

I can't understand a single word
δεν καταλαβαίνω τίποτε
then katalaveno tipote

can you get an interpreter?
μπορείτε να βρείτε έναν διερμηνέα;
borite na vrite enan thi-ermine-a?

the toilet won't flush
χάλασε το καζανάκι της τουαλέτας
Halasse to kazanaki tiss too-aletass

there's no plug in the bath
δεν έχει τάπα στην μπανιέρα
then eHi tapa stin bani-era

there's no hot water
δέν έχει ζεστό νερό
then eHi zesto nero

there's no toilet paper left
τελείωσε το χαρτί στην τουαλέτα
teliosse to Harti stin too-aleta

PROBLEMS

I'm afraid I've accidentally broken the . . .
χίλια συγνώμη, αλλά κατά λάθος έσπασα το . . .
Hilia siGnomi ala kata laτHoss espassa to . . .

this man has been following me
αυτός εδώ με ακολουθεί
aftoss etho me akolooτHi

I've been mugged
με κλέψανε
me klepsane

my handbag has been stolen
μου κλέψανε την τσάντα
moo klepsane tin tsanda

απαγορεύεται . . .	no . . .
αστυνομία	police
γραφείο απωλεσθέντων	lost property
δεν λειτουργεί	out of order
έξοδος κινδύνου	emergency exit
κίνδυνος!	danger!
κίνδυνος πυρκαγιάς	danger of fire
κίνδυνος κατολισθήσεων	danger of landslides
κίνδυνος ηλεκτροπληξίας	danger – high voltage
οδική βοήθεια	motorway assistance
προσοχή!	caution!
πρώτες βοήθειες	first aid
πυροσβεστήρας	fire extinguisher
πυροσβεστική υπηρεσία	fire brigade
φαρμακείο	chemist's

bandage	ο επίδεσμος *o epithesmoss*
blood	το αίμα *to ema*
broken	σπασμένο *spasmeno*
burn	το έγκαυμα *to eng-gavma*
chemist's	το φαρμακείο *to farmakio*
contraceptive	το προφυλακτικό *to profilaktiko*
dentist	ο οδοντίατρος *o othondiatross*
disabled	ανάπηρος *anapiross*
disease	η αρρώστια *i arostia*
doctor	ο γιατρός *o yatross*
health	η υγεία *i iyia*
hospital	το νοσοκομείο *to nossokomio*
ill	άρρωστος *arostoss*
nurse	η νοσοκόμα *i nossokoma*
wound	η πληγή *i pliyi*

I don't feel well
δεν νιώθω καλά
then niотно kala

it's getting worse
πάει χειρότερα
pa-i нirotera

I feel better
νιώθω καλύτερα
niотно kalitera

I feel sick
νιώθω άσχημα
niотно asнiма

I've got a pain here
έχω έναν πόνο εδώ
eно enan pono etho

it hurts
πονάει
pona-i

45

HEALTH

he's got a high temperature
έχει πυρετό
eHi pireto

could you call a doctor?
μπορείτε να φωνάξτε έναν γιατρό;
borite na fonaksete enan yatro?

is it serious?
είναι σοβαρό;
ine sovaro?

will he need an operation?
θα χρειαστεί εγχείρηση;
THA Hriasti enHirissi?

I'm diabetic
έχω ζάχαρο
eHo zaHaro

keep her warm
προσοχή να μην κρυώσει
prosoHi na min kriossi

have you got anything for ...?
έχετε τίποτε για ...;
eHete tipote ya ...?

αλοιφή	ointment
ανακινήσατε πριν από την χρήση	shake before use
δηλητήριο	poison
ιατρείο	surgery
παυσίπονο	painkiller
πριν από το φαγητό	before meals
πρώτες βοήθειες	first aid
σιρόπι	cough mixture
φαρμακείο	chemist's
... φορές την ημέρα	... times a day
χάπια	pills
χρήσις εξωτερική	external use only

SPORT

I want to learn to sailboard
θέλω να μάθω να κάνω σερφ
THelo na matho na kano surf

can we hire a sailing boat?
μπορούμε να νοικιάσουμε σκάφος για ιστιοπλοΐα;
boroome na nikiassoome skafoss ya istioplo-ia?

how much is half an hour's waterskiing?
πόσο κάνει το θαλάσσιο σκι, για μισή ώρα;
posso kani to THalassio ski ya missi ora?

can I hire a sailboard for two hours?
μπορώ να νοικιάσω ένα σερφ για δύο ώρες;
boro na nikiasso ena surf ya thio oress?

I'd like lessons in skin-diving
θέλω να κάνω μαθήματα για καταδύσεις
THelo na kano matHimata ya katathississ

can we use the tennis court?
μπορούμε να παίξουμε στο γήπεδο του τέννις;
boroome na peksoome sto yipetho too tenis?

I'd like to go and watch a football match
θα ήθελα να πάω σε κανένα ποδοσφαιρικό ματς
THa itHela na pao se kanena pothosferiko match

we're sailing around the islands
κάνουμε τον γύρο των νησιών
kanoome ton yiro ton nission

we're going to do some hill-walking
θα πάμε για ορειβασία
THa pame ya orivassia

this is the first time I've ever tried it
είναι η πρώτη φορά που προσπαθώ
ine i proti fora poo prospatHo

THE POST OFFICE

letter	το γράμμα *to Grama*
poste restante	η πόστ ρεστάντ *i post restand*
post office	το ταχυδρομείο *to taнidromio*
recorded delivery	συστημένο *sistimeno*
send	στέλνω *stelno*
stamp	το γραμματόσημο *to Gramatossimo*
telegram	το τηλεγράφημα *to tileGrafima*

how much is a letter to Ireland?
πόσο είναι να στείλω ένα γράμμα στην Ιρλανδία;
posso ine na stilo ena Grama stin irlanthia?

I'd like four . . . drachma stamps
θα ήθελα τέσσερα γραμματόσημα των . . . δραχμών
тна iтнela tessera Gramatossima ton . . . dhraнmon

I'd like six stamps for postcards to England
θα ήθελα έξι γραμματόσημα για κάρτες για την Αγγλία
тна iтнela eksi Gramatossima ya kartess ya tin anglia

is there any mail for me?
έχει κανένα γράμμα για μένα;
eнi kanena Grama ya mena?

I'm expecting a parcel from . . .
περιμένω ένα δέμα από . . .
perimeno ena thema apo . . .

αποστολέας	sender
γραμματόσημα	stamps
διεύθυνση	address
εξωτερικού	abroad
επιταγές	money orders
εσωτερικού	inland
συστημένα	registered letters
ταχυδρομικός κώδικας	post code

48

directory enquiries	οι πληροφορίες του ΟΤΕ *i pliroforiess too ote*
extension	η τηλεφωνική γραμμή *i tilefoniki ɢrami*
number	ο αριθμός *o ariтнmoss*
operator	η τηλεφωνήτρια *i tilefonitria*
phone (*verb*)	παίρνω τηλέφωνο *perno tilefono*
phone box	ο τηλεφωνικός θάλαμος *o tilefonikoss тнalamoss*
telephone	το τηλέφωνο *to tilefono*
telephone directory	ο τηλεφωνικός κατάλογος *o tilefonikoss katalocoss*

is there a phone round here?
υπάρχει τηλέφωνο εδώ κοντά;
iparнi tilefono etho konda?

can I use your phone?
μπορώ να πάρω ένα τηλέφωνο;
boro na paro ena tilefono?

I'd like to make a phone call to Britain
θα ήθελα να πάρω ένα τηλέφωνο στην Βρεταννία
тна iтнela na paro ena tilefono stin vretania

I want to reverse the charges
θέλω να ζητήσω να πληρώσει αυτός που καλώ
тнelo na zitisso na plirossi aftoss poo kalo

hello? (*answering*)
ναί;
ne?

could I speak to Anna?
μπορώ να μιλήσω στην Άννα, σας παρακαλώ;
boro na miliso stin Anna sass parakalo?

hello, this is Simon speaking
γειά σας, ο Σάιμον είμαι
ya sass o Simon ime

49

TELEPHONING

can I leave a message?
μπορώ να αφήσω ένα μήνυμα;
boro na afisso ena minima?

do you speak English?
μιλάτε Αγγλικά;
milate anglika?

could you say that again very very slowly?
μπορείτε να το ξαναπείτε αυτό πολύ πολύ αργά;
borite na to ksanapite afto poli poli arɕa?

could you tell him Jim called?
μπορείτε να του πείτε ότι πήρε ο Τζιμ;
borite na too pite oti pire o Jim?

could you ask her to ring me back?
μπορείτε να της πείτε να με πάρει;
borite na tiss pite na me pari?

I'll call back later
θα πάρω αργότερα
тна paro arɕotera

76 32 11
εβδομήντα έξι, τριάντα δύο, ένδεκα
evthominda eksi, trianda thio, entheka

just a minute please
ένα λεπτό σας παρακαλώ
ena lepto sass parakalo

he's not in
δεν είναι εδώ
then ine etho

sorry, I've got the wrong number
με συγχωρείτε, λάθος
me sinhorite laтнoss

it's engaged
μιλάει
mila-i

it's a terrible line
είναι πολύ άσχημη η γραμμή
ine poli asнimi i ɕrami

TELEPHONING

REPLIES

mia stiGmi
μια στιγμή
hang on

pioss na po oti ine?
ποιός να πω ότι είναι;
who shall I say is calling?

pioss ine?
ποιός είναι;
who's calling?

o ithioss
ο ίδιος
speaking

how do you spell it?
πώς το γράφεις;
poss to Grafiss?

I'll spell it
θα σου πω πώς γράφετε
THa soo poss Grafete

If you want to spell your own name then you can use the ordinary English pronunciation of the roman alphabet — which most Greeks will understand. For the Greek alphabet see page 4.

100	emergency (999)
131	directory enquiries
ακουστικό	receiver
αριθμός τηλεφώνου	phone number
διεθνές	international call
μετρητής	unit counter
μονάδα	unit
νόμισμα	coin
Ο.Τ.Ε.	Greek Telecom
τηλέφωνο	telephone
τηλεφωνικός θάλαμος	phone box
τηλεφωνικός κατάλογος	phone book
υπεραστικό	long-distance call

NUMBERS, THE DATE, THE TIME

0	μηδέν *mithen*
1	ένα *ena*
2	δύο *thio*
3	τρία *tria*
4	τέσσερα *tessera*
5	πέντε *pende*
6	έξι *eksi*
7	επτά *epta*
8	οκτώ *okto*
9	εννιά *enia*
10	δέκα *theka*
11	ένδεκα *entheka*
12	δώδεκα *thotheka*
13	δεκατρία *thekatria*
14	δεκατέσσερα *thekatessera*
15	δεκαπέντε *thekapende*
16	δεκαέξι *thekaeksi*
17	δεκαεπτά *thekaepta*
18	δεκαοκτώ *theka-okto*
19	δεκαεννιά *theka-enia*
20	είκοσι *ikossi*
21	εικοσιένα *ikossiena*
22	εικοσιδύο *ikossithio*
30	τριάντα *trianda*
35	τριάντα πέντε *triandapende*
40	σαράντα *saranda*
50	πενήντα *penida*
60	εξήντα *eksinda*
70	εβδομήντα *evthominda*
80	ογδόντα *ogthonda*
90	ενενήντα *eneninda*
100	εκατό *ekato*

NUMBERS, THE DATE, THE TIME

101	εκατόν ένα *ekato ena*

200	διακόσια *thiakossia*
300	τριακόσια *triakossia*
400	τετρακόσια *tetrakossia*
500	πεντακόσια *pendakossia*
600	εξακόσια *eksakossia*
700	επτακόσια *eptakossia*
800	οκτακόσια *oktakossia*
900	εννιακόσια *eniakossia*

1,000	χίλια ʜilia
2,000	δύο χιλιάδες *thio* ʜiliathess

7,550	επτά χιλιάδες πεντακόσια πενήντα
	epta ʜiliathess *pendakossia penida*

1,000,000	ένα εκατομμύριο *ena ekatomirio*

1st	πρώτος *protoss*
2nd	δεύτερος *thefteross*
3rd	τρίτος *tritoss*
4th	τέταρτος *tetartoss*
5th	πέμπτος *pemtoss*
6th	έκτος *ektoss*
7th	έβδομος *evthomoss*
8th	όγδοος οʜtho-oss
9th	έννατος *enatoss*
10th	δέκατος *thekatoss*

what's the date?
τι ημερομηνία είναι;
ti imerominia ine?

it's the 12th of January 1994
είνα δώδεκα Ιανουαρίου χίλια εννιακόσια ενενήντα
τέσσερα
ine thotheka lanoo-arioo ʜilia *eniakossia eneninda tessera*

what time is it?
τί ώρα είναι;
ti ora ine?

NUMBERS, THE DATE, THE TIME

it's midday/midnight
είναι μεσημέρι/μεσάνυχτα
ine messimeri/messanihta

it's one/three o'clock
είναι μία/τρεις η ώρα
ine mia/triss i ora

it's half past eight
είναι οκτώ και μισή
ine okto ke missi

it's a quarter past/to five
είναι πέντε και τέταρτο
ine pende ke tetarto

it's a quarter to five
είναι πέντε παρά τέταρτο
ine pende para tetarto

it's ten past seven
είναι επτά και δέκα
ine epta ke theka

it's twenty to nine
είναι εννιά παρά είκοσι
ine enia para ikossi

it's six a.m./p.m.
είναι έξι το πρωί/το απόγευμα
ine eksi to proi/to apo-yevma

at two/five p.m.
στις δύο/στις πεντε το απόγευμα
stis thio/stis pende to apo-yevma

a enass, mia, ena (*see grammar*)
about (*approx*) peripoo
above pano apo, apo pano
abroad sto eksoteriko
accelerator to gazi
accent i profora
accept theHome
accident to thistiHima
accommodation i thiamoni
accompany sinothevo
ache o ponoss
adaptor (*plug*) i priza taf
address i thi-efTHinsi
address book i adzenda ton
thi-efTHinseon
adult o enilikoss
advance: in advance
prokatavolika
advise simvoolevo
Aegean to E-yeo
aeroplane to a-eroplano
afraid: I'm afraid (of) fovame
after meta
afternoon apo-yevma
aftershave i kolonia meta to
ksirisma
afterwards meta
again ksana
against enadion
age i ilikia
agency to praktorio
agent o andiprossoposs
aggressive epiTHetikoss
ago prin; **three days ago**
prin triss meress
agree: I agree simfono
AIDS to 'AIDS'
air o a-erass
air: by air a-eroporikoss
air-conditioned
klimatizomenoss
air-conditioning o
klimatismoss
air hostess i a-erossinoTHoss
airline i a-eroporiki eteria
airmail: by airmail
a-eroporikoss
airport to a-erotTHromio
alarm o sina-yermoss
alarm clock to ksipnitiri
Albania i Alvania
alcohol to alko-ol
alive zodanoss
all ola; **all the milk/beer** olo
to Gala/oli i bira; **all day** oli
mera
allergic to aleryikoss se
all-inclusive ola pliromena
allow epitrepo
allowed epitrepete
all right: that's all right
endaksi
almost sHethon
alone monoss
already ithi
also epississ
alternator o enalaktirass
although an ke
altogether sinolika
always panda
a.m.: at 5 a.m. stiss pende to
pro-i

55

ambulance to asthenoforo
America i Ameriki
American Amerikanoss
among anamessa
amp: 13-amp 13 amber
ancestor o proGonoss
anchor i angira
ancient arheoss
and ke
angina i stithanhi
angry thimomenoss
animal to zo-o
ankle o astraGaloss
anniversary (*wedding*) i
  epetioss too Gamoo
annoying enohlitikoss
anorak to anorak
another aloss; **another beer**
  ali mia bira
answer i apandissi
answer (*verb*) apando
ant to mirmigi
antibiotic to adiviotiko
antifreeze to adipsiktiko
antihistamine to adi-
  istaminiko farmako
antique: it's an antique ine
  antika
antique shop to paleopolio
antiseptic to adissiptiko
**any: have you got any
  butter/bananas?** ehete
  katholoo vootiro/bananess?;
  I don't have any then eho
  katholoo
anything otithipote
anyway oposs ke nane
apartment to thiamerisma
aperitif to aperitif
apologize zito siGnomi
appalling apessioss
appendicitis i skoliko-ithitiss
appetite i oreksi

apple to milo
apple pie i milopita
appointment to randevoo
apricot to verikoko
April o Aprilioss
archaeology i arheolo-yia
area i periohi
arm to heri
arrest silamvano
arrival i afiksi
arrive ftano
art i tehni
art gallery i pinakothiki
artificial tehnitoss
artist o kalitehniss
as (*since*) oss; **as beautiful as**
  tosso omorfoss osso
ashamed: I feel ashamed
  drepome
ashtray to tassaki
ask roto
asleep: she's asleep kimate
asparagus ta sparagia
aspirin i aspirini
asthma to asthma
astonishing ekpliktikoss
at: at the station ston
  stathmo; **at Betty's** stin
  Beti; **at 3 o'clock** stiss triss i
  ora
Athens i Athina
Atlantic o Atlandikoss
attack i epithessi
attractive elkistikoss
aubergine i melidzana
audience to akro-atirio
August o AvGoostoss
aunt i thia
Australia i Afstralia
Australian Afstraloss
Austria i Afstria
automatic aftomatoss
autumn to fthinoporo

awake ksipnioss
awful apessioss
axe to tsekoori
axle o aksonass

B

baby to moro
baby-sitter i 'baby-sitter'
bachelor o eryeniss
back pisso; (of body) i plati;
  at the back sto pisso
  meross; the back
  wheel/seat o pisso troHoss/i
  pisso THessi
backpack o sakoss
bacon to 'bacon'
bad kakoss
badly asHima
bag i tsanda; (suitcase) i
  valitsa
bake psino
baker's o psomass
balcony to balkoni
bald. falakross
ball i bala; (small) to balaki
banana i 'banana'
bandage o epithesmoss
bank i trapeza
bar to 'bar'
barber o koore-ass
barmaid i servitora
barman o 'barman'
basement to ipo-yio
basket to kalaTHi
bath to banio
bathing cap to skoofaki too
  banioo
bathroom to lootro
bathtub i bani-era

battery i bataria
be ime (see grammar)
beach i paralia
beans ta fassolia; green
  beans ta fassolakia
beard ta yenia
beautiful oreoss
because epithi
because of eks etiass
become yinome
bed to krevati;
  single/double bed to
  mono/thiplo krevati; go to
  bed pao ya ipno
bed linen ta sedonia
bedroom to ipnothomatio
bee i melissa
beef to mosHari
beer i bira
before prin
begin arHizo
beginner o arHarioss
beginning i arHi
behind pisso
beige bez
Belgium to Velyio
believe pistevo
bell i kabana; (for door) to
  koothooni
belong aniko
below apo kato, kato apo
belt i zoni
bend i strofi
best: the best o kaliteross
better kaliteross; better
  than kaliteross apo
between metaksi
bicycle to pothilato
big meGaloss
bikini to 'bikini'
bill o loGariasmoss
bird to pooli
biro (R) to stilo

birthday ta yeneтнlia;
 happy birthday! нronia
 pola!
biscuit to biskoto
bit: a little bit liGo
bite (*insect*) to tsibima
bitter pikross
black mavross
black and white mavro-aspross
blackberry to vatomooro
bladder i kisti
blanket i kooverta
bleach to нarpik (*R*)
bleed emoraGo
bless you! ya soo!
blind tifloss
blister i fooskala
blocked frakarismenoss
blond ksantнoss
blood to ema
blood group i omatha
 ematoss
blouse i blooza
blow-dry to steGnoma malion
blue ble
boarding pass i karta
 epivivasseoss
boat to plio
body to soma
boil (*water*) vrazo
bomb i vomva
bone to kokalo
bonnet (*car*) to kapo
book to vivlio
book: book a seat klino
 тнessi
bookshop to vivliopolio
boot (*shoe*) i bota; (*car*) to
 port-bagaz
border ta sinora
boring varetoss
born: I was born in 1963
 yeniтнika to 1963

borrow thanizome
boss to afendiko
both: both of them ke i thio
bottle to bookali
bottle-opener to aniнtiri
bottom o viтнoss; (*of body*) o
 koloss; **at the bottom of** sto
 vaтнoss
bowl to bol
box to kooti
box office to tamio
boy to aGori
boyfriend o filoss
bra to sooti-en
bracelet to vraнioli
brake to freno
brake (*verb*) frenaro
brandy to koniak
brave yeneoss
bread psomi;
 white/wholemeal bread to
 aspro/mavro psomi
break spao
breakdown (*car*) i vlavi;
 (*nervous*) o nevrikoss
 klonismoss
breakfast to pro-ino
breast to stiтнoss
breastfeed vizeno
breathe anapneo
brick to toovlo
bridge (*over river etc*) i yefira
briefcase o нartofilakass
bring ferno
Britain i Vretania
British Vretanoss
brochure to prospektooss
broke: I'm broke ime
 apendaross
broken spasmenoss
brooch i karfitsa
brother o atherfoss
brother-in-law o Gambross

brown kafe
bruise i melania
brush i voortsa
bucket o koovass
building to ktirio
bulb (*light*) i lamba
Bulgaria i Voolgaria
bull o tavross
bumper o profilaktirass
bunk beds i kooketess
buoy i simathoora
burn to kapsimo
burn (*verb*) keo
bus to leoforio
business i thooli-ess
business trip to taksithi ya
  thooli-ess
bus station to praktorio
  leoforion
bus stop i stassi leoforioo
busy (*street, restaurant*)
  polissiнnastoss; (*person*)
  apasнolimenoss
but ala
butcher's o нassapiss
butter to vootiro
butterfly i petalootha
button to koobi
buy aгorazo
by: by car me aftokinito

C

cabbage to laнano
cabin (*ship*) i kabina
cable car to teleferik
café to kafenio
cake to 'cake'
cake shop to zaнaroplastio
calculator to kobiooteraki

calendar to imerolo-yio
call fonazo
calm down iremo
Calor gas (*R*) to iгra-erio
camera i fotoгrafiki miнani;
  (*movie*) i kinimatoгrafiki
  miнani
campbed to randzo
camping i kataskinossi
campsite to kambing
can (*tin*) to kooti
can: I/she can boro/bori; **can
  you ...?** borite na ...?;
  (*familiar*) boriss na ...?
Canada o Kanathass
Canadian Kanathoss
canal to kanali
cancel akirono
candle to keri
canoe to kano
cap (*head*) to kapelo; (*bottle*)
  to kapaki
captain (*ship*) o kapetanioss;
  (*plane*) o kivernitiss
car to aftokinito
caravan to troнospito
carburettor to karbirater
card (*business*) i karta;
  playing cards ta нartia
cardboard to нartoni
cardigan i zaketa
car driver o othiгoss
care: take care of prosseнo
careful prossektikoss; **be
  careful!** prosseнe!
car park to parking
carpet to нali; (*fitted*) i
  moketa
car rental i enikiassi
  aftokiniton
carriage (*train*) to vaгoni
carrot to karoto
carry metafero

carry-cot to port-be-be
cash: in cash tiss metritiss
cash desk to tamio
cassette i kasseta
cassette player to
  kassetofono
castle to kastro
cat i Gata
catch (ball etc) piano; where
  do we catch . . .? (bus etc)
  apo poo THa paroome . . .?
cathedral o kaTHethrikoss
  naoss
Catholic kaTHolikoss
cauliflower to koonoopithi
cause i etia
cave i spilia
ceiling to tavani
cemetery to nekrotafio
centigrade Kelsioo
central heating i kedriki
  THermansi
centre to kendro
century o eonass
certificate to pistopi-itiko
chain i alissitha
chair i karekla
chambermaid i kamari-era
chance: by chance kata tiHi
change (small) ta psila
change (buses, clothes) alazo
changeable (weather) astatoss
charter flight i ptissi tsarter
cheap ftinoss
check (verb) elenHo
check-in to 'check-in'
cheers! (toast) stin iya sass
cheese to tiri
chemist's to farmakio
cheque i epita-yi
cheque book to karne
  epitaGon
cheque card i karta epitaGon

cherry to kerassi
chest to stiTHoss
chestnut to kastano
chewing gum i tsiHla
chicken to kotopoolo
child to pethi
children ta pethia
children's portion i pethiki
  meritha
chin to piGooni
chips i tiGanitess patatess
chocolate i sokolata; milk
  chocolate i sokolata
  Galaktoss; hot chocolate i
  zesti sokolata
choke (on car) o aerass
choose thialeGo
chop (meat) i brizola
Christian name to mikro
  onoma
Christmas ta Hristooyena
church i eklissia
cigar to pooro
cigarette to tsiGaro
cinema to sinema
city i poli
city centre to kendro tiss poliss
class: first class proti THessi;
  second class thefteri THessi
classical music i klassiki
  moossiki
clean (adjective) kaTHaross
clean (verb) kaTHarizo
cleansing cream Galaktoma
  kaTHarismoo
clear (obvious) profaness
clever eksipnoss
cliff o apotomoss vraHoss
climate to klima
cloakroom (coats) i Gardaroba
clock to rolo-i
close (verb) klino
closed klistoss

ENGLISH-GREEK

clothes ta rooна
clothes peg to mandalaki
cloud to sinefo
cloudy sinefiasmenoss
club i lesнi
clutch o siblektiss
coach to poolman
coast i akti
coat (overcoat etc) to palto;
  (jacket) to sakaki
coathanger i kremastra
cockroach i katsaritha
cocktail to 'cocktail'
cocoa to kakao
coffee o kafess; white
  coffee o kafess me Gala
cold krioss; it's cold kani
  krio
cold (illness) to krioma; I've
  got a cold ime kriomenoss
cold cream i krema prossopoo
collar o yakass
collection (of antiques etc) i
  siloyi
colour to нroma
colour film to eнromo film
comb i нtena
come erнome; come back
  yirno; come in! peraste
comfortable anapaftikoss
company i eteria
compartment to koope
compass i piksitha
complain paraponoome
complicated berthemenoss
compliment i filofronissi
computer o ipolo-yistiss
concert i sinavlia
conditioner to kodissioner
condom to profilaktiko
confirm epiveveono
congratulations! siнaritiria!
connection (travel) i

andapokrissi
constipated: I am
  constipated eнo thiskilia
consulate to proksenio
contact (verb) erнome se epafi
contact lenses i faki epafiss
contraceptive pill to
  adissiliptiko
cook (man) o ma-yiross;
  (woman) i ma-yirissa
cook (verb) ma-yirevo
cooker i koozina
cooking utensils ta ma-yirika
  skevi
cool throsseross
Corfu i Kerkira
corkscrew to aniнtiri
corner i Gonia
correct sostoss
corridor o thiathromoss
cosmetics ta kalindika
cost: what does it cost? posso
  kani?
cot i koonia
cotton vamvakero
cotton wool to vamvaki
couchette i kooketa
cough o viнass
country i нora
countryside i eksoнi
course: of course vevea
cousin (male) o ksathelfoss;
  (female) i ksathelfi
cow i a-yelatha
crab to kavoori
crafts i нiroteнnia
cramp i kramba
crankshaft o strofaloss
crash i sigroossi
crayfish i karavitha
cream i krema
credit card i pistotiki karta
Crete i Kriti

61

ENGLISH-GREEK

crew to pliroma
crisps ta tsips
crockery ta piatika
cross (verb) perno
crowd o kosmoss
crowded yematoss kosmo
cruise i krooazi-era
crutches i pateritsess
cry kleo
cucumber to agoori
cup to flidzani
cupboard to doolapi
curtain i koortina
custom to еthimo
customs to telonio
cut (verb) kovo
cutlery ta maнeropiroona
cycling i pothilassia
cyclist o pothilatiss
Cyprus i Kipross

dad o babass
damage i zimia
damp igross
dance (verb) нorevo
danger o kinthinoss
dangerous epikinthinoss
dare tolmo
dark skotinoss
dashboard to kadran
date (time) i imerominia
dates (to eat) i нoormathess
daughter i kori
daughter-in-law i nifi
day i mera; the day before
  yesterday proнtess; the
  day after tomorrow
  meтнavrio

dead peтнamenoss
deaf koofoss
dear aгapitoss; (expensive)
  akrivoss
death o тнanatoss
decaffeinated нoriss kafe-ini
December o Thekemvrioss
decide apofassizo
deck to katastroma
deckchair i sez long
deep vaтнiss
delay i kaтнisterissi
deliberately epitithess
delicious nostimotatoss
demand apeto
dentist o othondo-yatross
dentures i massela
deodorant to aposmitiko
department store to meгalo
  katastima
departure i anaнorissi
depend: it depends eksartate
depressed тнlimenoss
dessert to гlikisma
develop (film) emfanizo
device to miнanima
diabetic o thiavitikoss
dialect i thialektoss
dialling code o kothikoss
  ariтнmoss
diamond to thiamandi
diarrhoea i thiaria
diary to imerolo-yi-o
dictionary to leksiko
die peтнeno
diesel (fuel) to dizel
diet i thi-eta
different thiaforetikoss
difficult thiskoloss
dining car to vaгoni
  estiatorioo
dining room i trapezaria
dinner to thipno

62

dinner: have dinner tro-o
vrathino
direction i katefтнinsi
directory enquiries i
plirofori-ess
dirty vromikoss
disabled anapiross
disappear eksafanizome
disappointed apoGo-
itevmenoss
disaster i katastrofi
disco i diskotek
disease i arostia
disgusting apessioss
dish to piato
disinfectant to apolimandiko
distance i apostassi
distributor (*in car*) to
distribiter
district (*in town*) i sinikia
disturb enoнlo
dive vooto
divorced нorismenoss
do kano; **that'll do nicely**
ola kala
doctor o yatross
document to enGrafo
dog o skiloss
doll i kookla
donkey o Ga-ithaross
door i porta
double thiplo
double room to thiplo
thomatio
down: down there eki kato;
I feel a bit down then
nioтнo poli kala
downstairs kato
draught to revma
dream to oniro
dress to forema
dress (*someone*) dino; (*self*)
dinome

dressing gown i roba
drink to poto
drink (*verb*) pino
drinking water to possimo
nero
drive othiGo
driver o othiGoss ·
driving licence i athia
othiyisseoss
drop i staGona
drop (*verb*) riнno
drugs (*narcotic*) ta narkotika
drunk meтнismenoss
dry steGnoss; (*wine*) ksiross
dry (*verb*) steGnono
dry-cleaner to steGno-
kaтнaristirio
duck i papia
durex (*R*) to profilaktiko
during kata ti thiarkia
dustbin o skoopithodenekess
Dutch Olanthoss
duty-free ta aforolo-yita
duty-free shop to katastima
aforolo-yiton

each kaтнe; **each one** o
kaтнenass
ear to afti
early noriss; (*too early*) poli
noriss
earn kerthizo
earrings ta skoolarikia
earth to нoma
east i anatoli; **east of**
anatolika apo
Easter to Pasнa
easy efkoloss
eat tro-o

eau de toilette i kolonia
edge i akri
egg to avGo; **hard-boiled egg** avGo sfiHto; **boiled egg** avGo vrasto
egg cup i avGOTHiki
either... or... i...i...
elastic elastikoss
Elastoplast (R) to lefkoplast (R)
elbow o angonass
electric ilektrikoss
electricity to ilektriko revma
else: something else kati alo
elsewhere aloo
embassy i presvia
emergency i ektati anagi
emergency exit i eksothoss kinthinoo
empty athioss
end to teloss
engaged (*toilet, phone*) katilimenoss; (*to be married*) aravoniasmenoss
engine i miHani; (*train*) i miHani
England i Aglia
English Aglikoss; (*language*) ta Aglika
English girl/woman i Aglitha
Englishman o Agloss
enlargement i me-yenTHissi
enough arketa; **that's enough** ftani
enter beno
entrance i issothoss
envelope o fakeloss
epileptic o epiliptikoss
especially ithika
Europe Évropi
European Evrope-ikoss
even: even men akoma ke i adress; **even if** akoma ki

an; **even more beautiful** akoma pio omorfoss
evening to vrathi; **good evening** kalispera
ever: have you ever ...? eHete pote ...?
every kaTHe; **every time** kaTHe fora; **every day** kaTHe mera
everyone oli
everything kaTHe ti
everywhere pandoo
exaggerate ipervalo
example to parathiGma; **for example** parathiGmatoss Hari
excellent eksoHoss
except ektoss
excess baggage to ipervaro
exchange andalasso
exchange rate i sinalaGmatiki issotimia
exciting sinarpastikoss
excuse me siGnomi
exhaust i eksatmissi
exhibition i ekTHessi
exit i eksothoss
expensive akrivoss
explain eksiGo
extension lead i pro-ektassi
eye to mati
eyebrow to frithi
eyeliner to 'eye-liner'
eye shadow i skia mation

face to prossopo
factory to erGostassio

faint (*verb*) lipoTHimo
fair (*funfair*) to paniyiri
fair (*adjective*) thikeoss
fall pefto
false pseftikoss
family i iko-yenia
famous thiassimoss
fan o anemistirass
fan belt to loori too
  vendilater
fantastic fandastikoss
far (*away*) makria
farm to aGroktima
farmer o aGrotiss
fashion i motha
fashionable tiss mothass
fast GriGoross
fat (*adjective*) paHiss
fat to paHoss
father o paterass
father-in-law o peTHeross
fault: it's my/it's his fault
  eGo fteo/aftoss fte-i
faulty elatomatikoss
favourite aGapimenoss
fear o fovoss
February o Fevrooarioss
fed up: I'm fed up with eHo
  vareTHi me
feel: I feel well nioTHo kala;
  I don't feel well then
  nioTHo kala; **I feel like ...**
  THa iTHela ...
feeling to sinesTHima
felt-tip pen o markathoross
feminist i feministria
fence to fraktiss
ferry to ferri bot
fever o piretoss
few: few tourists liyi
  tooristess; **a few** liGa
fiancé o aravoniastikoss
fiancée i aravoniastikia

field to Horafi
fight i aGonass
fight (*verb*) malono
fill yemizo
fillet to fileto
filling (*tooth*) to sfra-yisma
film to film
filter to filtro
find vrisko
fine to prostimo
fine omorfoss; (*weather*)
  oreoss
finger to thaHtilo
fingernail to niHi
finish teliono
fire i fotia; (*blaze*) i pirka-yia
fire brigade i pirosvestiki
  ipiressia
fire extinguisher o
  pirosvestirass
fireworks ta piroteHnimata
first protoss; (*firstly*) prota
first aid i protess vo-iTHi-ess
first class (*travel*) proti THessi
first floor to proto patoma
first name to onoma
fish to psari
fishing to psarema
fishmonger's to psarathiko
fit (*healthy*) yimnasmenoss
fizzy me anTHrakiko
flag i sime-a
flash to flass
flat to thiamerisma
flat (*adjective*) epipethoss
flat (tyre) skasmeno lastiHo
flavour i yefsi
flea o psiloss
flight i ptissi
flirt flertaro
floor (*of room*) to patoma;
  (*storey*) o orofoss
florist o anTHopoliss

ENGLISH-GREEK

flour to alevri
flower to looloothi
flu i Gripi
fly i miGa
fly (verb) peto
fog i omiHli
folk music i thimotiki
  moossiki
follow akolooTHo
food to fa-yito
food poisoning trofiki
  thilitiriassi
foot to pothi; feet ta pothia;
  on foot me ta pothia
football to pothosfero
for ya
forbidden apaGorevmenoss
forehead to metopo
foreigner o ksenoss
forest to thassoss
forget kseHno
fork to pirooni; (in road) i
  thiaklathossi
fortnight theka-penTHimero
fortunately eftiHoss
fountain i piyi
fracture to kataGma
France i Galia
free elefTHeross; (of charge)
  thore-an
freezer i katapsiksi
French Galikoss; (language)
  ta Galika
fresh freskoss
Friday i Paraskevi
fridge to psiyio
friend o filoss
from: from Rhodes to Athens
  apo tin Rotho stin ATHina
front (part) to brostino
  meross; in front of brosta
  apo
frost o pa-yetoss

fruit ta froota
fry tiGanizo
frying pan to tiGani
full yematoss
full board fool pansion
fun: have fun! kali
  thiaskethassi!
funeral i kithia
funnel (for pouring) to Honi
funny (strange) paraksenoss;
  (amusing) astioss
furious poli THimomenoss
furniture ta epipla
further parapera
fuse i asfalia
future to melon

G

game (to play) to peHnithi;
  (meat) to kiniyi
garage (parking) to garaz;
  (repair) to sineryio; (fuel)
  to venzinathiko
garden o kiposs
garlic to skortho
gas to gazi
gas permeable lenses i
  imiskliri faki epafiss
gate (airport) i eksothoss
gauge o thiktiss
gay omofilofiloss
gear (car) o taHitita;
  (equipment) ta praGmata
gearbox to kivotio taHititon
gear lever o levi-ess taHititon
gentleman o kirioss
gents (toilet) i tooalèta ton
  anthron
genuine afTHendikoss

66

ENGLISH-GREEK

German Yermanikoss;
(*language*) ta Yermanika
Germany i Yermania
get (*fetch*) perno; **can you tell
me how to get to ...?** borite
na moo pite poss na pao sto
...?; **get back** (*return*)
yirno pisso; **get in** (*car*)
aneveno; **get off**
kateveno; **get up**
sikonome; **get out!** ekso!
gin to tzin
gin and tonic to tzin me tonik
girl to koritsi
girlfriend i filenatha
give thino; **give back**
epistrefo
glad efHaristimenoss
glass (*substance*) to yali;
(*drinking*) to potiri
glasses ta yalia
gloves ta Gandia
glue i kola
go pao; **go in** beno; **go out**
v-yeno; **go down**
kateveno; **go up** aneveno;
go through thiasHizo; **go
away** fevGo; **go away!** fiye!
goat i katsika
God o THeoss
goddess i THe-a
gold o Hrissoss
golf to golf
good kaloss; **good!** kala!
goodbye adio
goose i Hina
got: have you got ...? eHete
...?; (*familiar*) eHiss ...?
government i kivernissi
grammar i Gramatiki
grandfather o papooss
grandmother i ya-ya
grapefruit to 'grapefruit'

grapes ta stafilia
grass to Hortari
grateful evGnomon
greasy lipaross
Greece i Elatha
Greek Elinikoss; (*man*) o
Elinass; (*woman*) i Elinitha;
(*language*) ta Elinika
green prassinoss
greengrocer o manaviss
grey grizoss
grilled psitoss sti sHara
grocer's to bakaliko
ground floor to isso-yio
group to groop
guarantee i engi-issi
guest o filoksenoomenoss
guesthouse i pansion
guide o ksenaGoss
guidebook o tooristikoss
othiGoss
guitar i kiTHara
gun (*pistol*) to pistoli; (*rifle*)
to oplo

habit i siniTHia
hair ta malia
haircut to koorema
hairdresser i komotria
hair dryer to pistolaki
hair lacquer i lak
half missoss; **half a
litre/day** misso litro/missi
mera; **half an hour** missi
ora
half board demi-pansion
ham to zambon
hamburger to Hamboorger

hammer to sfiri
hand to Heri
handbag i tsanda
handbrake to Hirofreno
handkerchief to madili
handle to Herooli
hand luggage to sak-vwa-yaz
handsome oreoss
hanger i kremastra
happen simveni
happy eftiHismenoss; **happy
  Christmas!** kala
  Hristooyena!; **happy New
  Year!** eftiHismenoss o
  kenooryoss Hronoss!
harbour to limani
hard skliross; *(difficult)*
  thiskoloss
hard lenses i skliri faki
hat to kapelo
hate misso
have eHo; **I have to . . .**
  prepi na . . .
hay fever aler-yia sti yiri
hazelnut to foondooki
he aftoss *(see grammar)*
head to kefali
headache o ponokefaloss
headlights i provoliss
health: your health! stin iya
  soo!
healthy iyi-iss
hear akoo-o
hearing aid ta akoostika
heart i karthia
heart attack i karthiaki
  prosvoli
heat i zesti
heating i тHermansi
heavy variss
heel *(of foot)* i fterna; *(of shoe)*
  to takooni
helicopter to elikoptero

hello ya sass; *(familiar)* ya
  soo
help i voiтHia
help *(verb)* voiтHo
her *(possessive)* o/i/to . . . tiss;
  (object) tin *(see grammar)*
herbs votana
here etho; **here is/are** na
hers thiko tiss *(see grammar)*
hiccups o loksiGass
hide krivo; *(oneself)* krivome
high psiloss
highway code o kothikass
  kikloforiass
hill o lofoss
him ton *(see grammar)*
hip o Gofoss
hire: for hire enikiazete
his o/i/to . . . too; **it's his** ine
  thiko too *(see grammar)*
history i istoria
hit Htipo
hitchhike kano otostop
hitchhiking to otostop
hobby to Hobi
hold krato
hole i tripa
holiday i thiakopess;
  (public) i aryi-ess; **summer
  holidays** i kalokeriness
  thiakopess
Holland i Olanthia
home: at home sto spiti; **go
  home** yirno spiti
homemade spitissioss
homesick: I'm homesick
  nostalGo
honest timioss
honey to meli
honeymoon o minass too
  melitoss
hoover *(R)* i ilektriki skoopa
hope elpizo

horn to klakson
horrible friktoss
horse to aloGo
horse riding i ipassia
hospital to nossokomio
hospitality i filoksenia
hot zestoss; (*to taste*) kaftoss; (*spicy*) kafteross
hotel to ksenothoHio
hot-water bottle i THermofora
hour i ora
house to spiti
house wine to krassi too maGazioo
how? poss?; **how are you?** ti kaniss?; (*polite*) ti kanete?; **how are things?** poss pa-i?; **how many?** possi?; **how much?** posso kani?
humour to Hioomor
hungry: I'm hungry pino
hurry viazome; **hurry up!** viassoo!
hurt travmatizome
husband o siziGoss

I eGo (*see grammar*)
ice o paGoss
ice cream to paGoto
ice cube to paGaki
ice lolly to paGoto ksilaki
ID card i taftotita
idea i ithe-a
idiot o vlakass
if an
ignition i miza
ill arostoss
immediately amessoss

important spootheoss
impossible athinatoss
improve veltiono
in messa; **in London** sto Lonthino; **in Greece** stin Elatha; **in Greek** sta Elinika; **in 1945** to 1945; **is he in?** ine eki?
included siberilam-vanete
incredible apiTHanoss
independent aneksartitoss
indicator (*car*) to flass
indigestion i thispepsia
industry i viomiHania
infection i molinsi
information i plirofori-ess
information desk i plirofori-ess
injection i enessi
injured travmatismenoss
inner tube (*tyre*) i sabrela
innocent aTHo-oss
insect to endomo
insect repellent to AUTAN (*R*)
inside messa
insomnia i a-ipnia
instant coffee to neskafe
instructor o thaskaloss
insurance i asfalia
intelligent eksipnoss
interesting enthiaferon
introduce sistino
invitation i prosklissi
invite proskalo
Ireland i Irlanthia
Irish Irlanthoss
iron (*metal*) to sithero; (*for clothes*) to ilektriko sithero
iron (*verb*) sitherono
island to nissi
it afto; **it is . . .** ine . . .
Italian Italikoss

Italy i Italia
itch i faGoora
IUD to spiral

J

jack (*car*) o Griloss
jacket to sakaki
jam i marmelatha
January o I-anooarioss
jaw to saGoni
jazz i tzaz
jealous ziliariss
jeans ta tzins
jellyfish i tsooHtra
jeweller's to HrissoHo-io
jewellery ta kosmimata
Jew (*man*) o Evreoss;
  (*woman*) i Evre-a
job i thoolia
joint (*to smoke*) to strifto
joke to astio
journey to taksithi; **have a
  good journey!** kalo taksithi!
jug i kanata
juice o Himoss
July o I-oolioss
jump pitho
jumper to poolover
junction i thiastavrossi
June o I-oonioss
just: **just two** monon thio;
  just a little mono liGo

K

keep krato

key to klithi
kidneys ta nefra
kill skotono
kilo to kilo
kilometre to Hiliometro
kind evyenikoss
king o vassiliass
kiss to fili
kiss (*verb*) filo
kitchen i koozina
knee to Gonato
knife to maHeri
knit pleko
knock over anapotho-yirizo
know ksero; (*person*)
  Gnorizo; **I don't know**
  then ksero

L

label i etiketa
ladder i skala
ladies (*toilet*) i tooaleta ton
  yinekon
lady i kiria
lager i bira
lake i limni
lamb to arni
lamp i lamba
land (*verb*) apovivazome
landscape to topio
language i Glossa
language school i sHoli
  ksenon Glosson
large meGaloss
last telefteoss; **last year**
  persi; **at last!** epitelooss!
late arGa

later arɢotera
laugh yelo
laundry (to wash) i booɢatha; (place) to katharistirio
law o nomoss
lawn to ɢrassithi
lawyer o thikiɢoross
laxative to kathartiko
lazy tebeliss
leaf to filo
leaflet to thiafimistiko
leak i thiarro-i
learn matheno
least: at least toolahiston
leather to therma
leave (bag etc) afino; (go away) fevɢo; (forget) ksehno
left aristera
left: on the left sta aristera
left-handed aristerohirass
left luggage o hoross filaksiss aposkevon
leg to pothi
lemon to lemoni
lemonade i lemonatha
lemon tea to tsa-i me lemoni
lend thanizo
length to mikoss
lens o fakoss
less liɢotero
lesson to mathima
let (allow) epitrepo
letter to ɢrama
letterbox to ɢramatokivotio
lettuce to marooli
level crossing i issopethi thiavassi
library i vivliothiki
licence i athia
lid to kapaki
lie (say untruth) leo psemata
lie down ksaplono

life i zo-i
lift (elevator) to assanser; give a lift to piyeno
light (in room) to foss
light (adjective: not heavy) elafross; light blue anihto ble
light (verb) anavo; have you got a light? ehete fotia
light bulb i lamba
lighter o anaptirass
lighthouse o faross
light meter to fotometro
lights (on car) ta fota
like: I like it moo aressi; I would like ... tha ithela ...
like (as) san
lip to hili
lipstick to krayon
liqueur to liker
list o kataloɢoss
listen akoo-o
litre to litro
litter ta skoopithia
little mikross; a little bit (of) liɢo
live zo; (in town etc) meno
liver to sikoti
living room to kathistiko
lobster o astakoss
lock i klitharia
lock (verb) klithono
lollipop to ɢlifidzoori
London to Lonthino
long makriss; a long time poliss keross
look: look (at) kitazo; it looks (seems) miazi; look: look like miazi san; look for psahno; look out! prossekse!
lorry to fortiɢo

71

lose Hano
lost property office to Grafio apolesTHendon
lot: a lot (of) pola
loud thinatoss
lounge (*in hotel, airport*) to saloni
love i aGapi; (*sexual*) o erotass; **make love** kano erota
love (*verb*) aGapo
lovely oreoss
low Hamiloss
luck i tiHi; **good luck!** kali tiHi!
luggage i aposkevess
lukewarm Hliaross
lunch to yevma
lungs i pnevmoness

macho macho
mad treloss
Madam kiria
magazine to periothiko
maiden name to patriko
mail to taHithromio
main kirioss
make kano
make-up to 'make-up'
male chauvinist pig o falokratiss
man o andrass
manager o 'manager'
many pola
map i Hartiss
March o Martioss
margarine i marGarini
market i aGora

marmalade i marmelatha
married (*man*) padremenoss; (*woman*) padremeni
mascara i maskara
mass (*church*) i litooryia
match (*light*) to spirto; (*sport*) to mats
material to ifasma
matter: it doesn't matter then pirazi
mattress to stroma
May o Ma-ioss
maybe issoss
mayonnaise i ma-yoneza
me emena; **for me** ya emena; **me too** ki eGo epississ (*see grammar*)
meal to fa-yito; **enjoy your meal!** kali oreksi!
mean (*verb*) eno-o
measles i ilara; **German measles** i eriTHra
meat to kre-ass
mechanic o miHanikoss
medicine (*drug*) to farmako
Mediterranean i Messo-yioss
medium (*steak*) missopsimeno
medium-sized metrio meyeTHoss
meet sinando
meeting i sinadissi
melon to peponi
mend thiorTHono
menu to menoo; **set menu** tabl d'ot
message to minima
metal to metallo
metre to metro
midday to messimeri
middle i messi
midnight ta messaniHta
milk to Gala
minced meat o kimass

ENGLISH-GREEK

mind: do you mind if I ...?
THa se piraze an ...?
mine thiko moo (*see grammar*)
mineral water to metaliko
nero
minute to lepto
mirror o kaTHreftiss
Miss i thespinitha
miss (*train etc*) Hano; **I miss
you** moo lipiss
mistake to laTHoss
misunderstanding i
pareksiyissi
mix anakatevo
modern modernoss
moisturizer i ithatiki krema
Monday i theftera
money ta lefta
month o minass
monument (*statue*) to mnimio
mood i thiaTHessi
moon to fengari
moped to miHanaki
more perissotero; **some
more** akomi liGo
morning to pro-i; **good
morning** kalimera
mosquito to koonoopi
most (of) perissotero (apo)
mother i mitera
mother-in-law i peTHera
motorbike i motossikleta
motorboat i varka me miHani
motorway i eTHniki othoss
mountain to voono
mouse to pondiki
moustache to moostaki
mouth to stoma
move (*get something out of
way*) metakino; **move
house** alazo spiti
Mr o Kirioss
Mrs i Kiria

much poli
mum i mama
muscle o miss
museum to moossio
mushrooms ta manitaria
music i moossiki
musical instrument to
moossiko orGano
mussels ta mithia
must: I/she must ... prepi
na ...
mustard i moostartha
my o/i/to ... moo (*see
grammar*)

nail (*in wall*) to karfi
nail clippers o niHokoptiss
nailfile i lima niHion
nail polish to mano
nail polish remover to asseton
naked yimnoss
name to onoma; **what's your
name?** poss se lene?; **my
name is Jim** me lene Tzim
napkin i petseta
nappy i pana
nappy-liners ta 'Pampers' (R)
narrow stenoss
nationality i eTHnikotita
natural fissikoss
nature i fissi
near konda; **near here** etho
konda; **the nearest ...** to
pio kondino ...
nearly sHethon
necessary anageo
neck o lemoss
necklace to koli-e
need: I need ... Hriazome ...

73

needle i velona
negative (*film*) to arnitiko
neighbour o yitonass
neither ... nor ... oote ... oote ...
nephew o anipsioss
nervous nevrikoss
neurotic nevrotikoss
never pote
new neoss
news (*TV etc*) ta ne-a, i ithississ
newsagent o efimerithopoliss
newspaper i efimeritha
New Year to neo etoss
New Year's Day i protoнronia
next (*following*) epomenoss; next Wednesday tin ali Tetarti; next to thipla apo
nice (*person*) kaloss; (*place etc*) oreoss; (*food*) nostimoss
nickname to paratsookli
niece i anipsia
night i niнta; good night kaliniнta
nightclub to naitklab
nightdress to niнtiko
nightmare o efialtiss
no oнi; I have no ... then eно ...
nobody kanenass
noise i fassaria
noisy тнorivothiss
non-smoking mi kapnizondess
normal fissiolo-yikoss
north o vorass; north of voria apo
Northern Ireland i Voria Irlanthia
nose i miti
not then; I'm not tired then

ime koorasmenoss; not for me oнi ya mena
note (*money*) to нartonomisma
notebook to simiomatario
nothing tipote
novel to miтнistorima
November o No-emvrioss
now tora
nowhere pootнena
number o ariтнmoss
number plate i pinakithess
nurse i nossokoma
nut (*to eat*) to karithi; (*for bolt*) to paksimathi

obnoxious andipaтнitikoss
obvious profaniss
October o Oktovrioss
octopus to нtapothi
of too (*see grammar*)
off (*lights*) klisto
offend prosvalo
offer (*verb*) prosfero
office to Grafio
often siнna
oil (*for car*) ta lathia; (*on salad*) to lathi
ointment i alifi
OK endaksi
old (*person*) yeross; (*thing*) palioss; how old are you? posso нronon isse?; I'm 25 years old ime 25 нronon
old-age pensioner o sindaksiooнoss
olive i elia
olive oil to eleolatho

ENGLISH-GREEK

omelette i omeleta
on pano; (*lights*) aninto
once mia fora
one enass, mia, ena (*see grammar*)
onion to kremithi
only mono
open (*adjective*) aniktoss
open (*verb*) aniGo
opera i opera
operation i enHirissi
opposite apenandi; **opposite the church** apenandi apo tin eklissia
optician o optikoss
optimistic essiothoksoss
or i
orange to portokali
orange (*colour*) portokali
orchestra i orHistra
order (*in restaurant etc*) paragelno
organize orGanono
other aloss, ali, alo
otherwise thiaforetika
our o/i/to ...mass (*see grammar*)
ours thiko mass (*see grammar*)
out: **she's out** then ine etho, ine ekso
outside ekso
oven o foornoss
over (*above*) apo pano; (*finished*) teliossan; **over there** eki
overdone poli ma-yiremeno
overtake prosperno
owner o ithioktitiss
oyster to strithi

pack (*verb*) ftiaHno tiss valitsess
package to paketo
package tour i orGanomeni ekthromi
packet to paketo
page i selitha
pain o ponoss
painful othiniross
painkiller to pafsipono
paint (*walls*) vafo; (*pictures*) zoGrafizo
paint brush to pinelo
painting i zoGrafiki
pair to zevGari
palace to palati
pancake i krepa
panic o panikoss
panties to slip
paper to Harti
parcel to thema
pardon? siGnomi?
parents i Goniss
park to parko
park (*verb*) parkaro
part to meross
party (*celebration*) to parti; (*group*) i omatha
pass (*mountain*) to perasma
passenger o epivatiss
passport to thiavatirio
pasta ta zimarika
pâté to pate
path to monopati
pavement to pezothromio
pay plirono
peach to rothakino
peanuts ta fistikia
pear to aнlathi

ENGLISH-GREEK

peas ta bizelia
pedal to petali
pedestrian o pezoss
pedestrian crossing i
  thiavassi pezon
pedestrian precinct o
  pezothromoss
pen to stilo
pencil to molivi
pencil sharpener i ksistra
penicillin i penikilini
penis to peoss
penknife o sooyiass
people i anthropi, o
  kosmoss; not many people
  ohi poliss kosmoss
pepper (spice) to piperi;
  (vegetable) i piperia
per: per week tin
  evthomatha; per cent tiss
  ekato
perfect telioss
perfume to aroma
period i periothoss
perm i permanand
person to atomo
petrol i venzini
petrol station to
  venzinathiko
phone (verb) perno tilefono
phone book o tilefonikoss
  katalocoss
phone box o tilefonikoss
  thalamoss
phone number o arithmoss
  tilefonoo
photograph i fotografia
photograph (verb) vgazo
  fotografia
photographer o fotografoss
phrase book to vivlio
  thialocon
pickpocket o portofolass

picnic to piknik
piece to komati
pig to goorooni
piles (med) i emoro-ithess
pill to hapi
pillow to maksilari
pilot o pilotoss
pin i karfitsa
pineapple o ananass
pink roz
pipe o solinass; (to smoke) i
  pipa
pity: it's a pity ine krima
pizza i pitsa
plan to shethio
plane to a-eroplano
plant to fito
plastic plastikoss
plastic bag i plastiki sakoola
plate to piato
platform (station) i platforma
play (theatre) to theatriko
  ergo
play (verb) pezo
pleasant efharistoss
please parakalo
pleased efharistimenoss;
  pleased to meet you harika
pliers i pensa
plug (electrical) i briza; (in
  sink) i tapa
plum to thamaskino
plumber o ithravlikoss
p.m. m.m.; 3 p.m. 3 meta
  messimvriass; 11 p.m. 11
  to vrathi
pneumonia i pnevmonia
pocket i tsepi
poison to thilitirio
police i astinomia
policeman o astifilakass
police station to astinomiko
  tmima

76

polite evyenikoss
political politikoss
politics ta politika
polluted molismenoss
pond i limnoola
pony to poni
poor (*not rich*) ftoнoss;
  (*quality etc*) kakoss
pop music i moossiki pop
pork to нirino
porter o aн-тнofoross;
  (*doorman*) o тнiroross
portion i meritha
possible thinatoss
post (*verb*) taнithromo
post (*mail*) ta гramata
postcard i kartpostal
poster (*for room*) to poster;
  (*in street*) i afissa
poste restante post restand
postman o taнithromoss
post office to taнithromio
potato i patata
poultry ta poolerika
pound (*sterling*) i lira;
  (*weight*) i libra
power cut i thiakopi
practical praktikoss
pram to karotsaki
prawn i гaritha
prefer protimo
pregnant engioss
prepare etimazo
prescription i sinda-yi
present (*gift*) to thoro
pretty oreoss; **pretty good**
  arketa kala
price i timi
priest o papass
prince o pringipass
princess i pringipissa
printed matter endipa
prison i filaki

private ithiotikoss
probably piтнanoss
problem to provlima
programme to proгrama
prohibited: it's prohibited
  apaгorevete
promise (*verb*) iposнome
pronounce profero
protect prostatevo
Protestant o
  thiamartiromenoss
proud iperifanoss
public thimossioss
pull travo
pump i adlia
puncture to foo-it
punk pank
purple mov
purse to portofoli
push sproнno
pushchair i anapiriki
  poliтнrona
put vazo
pyjamas i pitzamess

quality i piotita
quarter to tetarto
quay i provlita
queen i vassilissa
question i erotissi
queue i oora
queue (*verb*) kano oora
quick(ly) гriгora
quiet issiнoss; **quiet!** siopi!
quilt to paploma
quite arketa

ENGLISH-GREEK

rabbit to kooneli
radiator to kalorifer; (*car*) to psiyio aftokinitoo
radio to rathiofono
railway o sithirothromoss
rain i vroHi
rain: it's raining vreHi
rainbow to ooranio tokso
raincoat i kabardina
rape o viasmoss
rare spanioss; (*steak*) oHi poli psimeno
raspberry to vatomooro
rat o arooreoss
rather malon
raw omoss
razor to ksirafaki; (*electric*) i ksiristiki miHani
razor blade to ksirafaki
read thiavazo
ready etimoss
really praGmatika
rear lights ta pisso fota
rearview mirror o kaTHreftiss aftokinitoo
receipt i apothiksi
receive theHome
reception (*hotel*) i ressepsion
receptionist i/o ressepsionist
recipe i sinda-yi
recognize anaGnorizo
recommend sistino
record o thiskoss
record player to pikap
record shop to thiskathiko
red kokinoss
red-headed kokinomaliss
refund (*verb*) thino pisso, apozimiono

relatives i sigeniss
relax ksekoorazome
religion i THriskia
remember THimame
rent to enikio
rent (*verb*) nikiazo; **to rent** enikiazete
repair i episkevi
repeat epanalamvano
reservation: I have a reservation eHo mia kratissi
reserve krato
responsible ipefTHinoss
rest (*remainder*) to ipolipo; (*sleep*) i anapafsi; **take a rest** anapavome
restaurant to estiatorio
return ticket to issitirio me epistrofi
reverse (*gear*) i opisTHen
reverse charge call to tilefonima kolekt
rheumatism i revmatismi
Rhodes i Rothoss
rib to plevro
rice to rizi
rich ploossioss; (*food*) variss
ridiculous yelioss
right (*side*) theksia; **on the right** (**of**) sta theksia; (*correct*) sostoss
right of way i protereotita
ring (*on finger*) to thaktilithi
ring (*phone*) tilefono
ripe orimoss
river to potami
road o thromoss; (*in town*) i othoss
roadsign i pinakitha
roadworks othika er-Ga
rock o vraHoss
rock music i rok
roll to psomaki

roof i steyi
roof rack i sHara aftokinitoo
room to thomatio
rope to sHini
rose to triadafilo
rotten (*fruit etc*) sapioss
round (*circular*) strongiloss
route i poria
rowing boat i varka me
    koopia
rubber (*material*) to lastiHo;
    (*eraser*) i svistra
rubber band to lastiHaki
rubbish ta skoopithia
rucksack to sakithio
rude a-yeniss
rug to Halaki
ruins i arHeotitess
rum to roomi
run treHo

sad lipimenoss
safe asfaliss
safety pin i paramana
sail to pani
sailboard to windsurf
sailing i istioplo-ia
sailing boat to istioplo-iko
    skafoss
salad i salata
salad dressing to lathoksitho
sale i polissi; (*reduced price*) i
    ekptossiss; for sale polite
salmon o solomoss
salt to alati
salty almiross
same: the same o ithioss
sand i amoss

sandals ta santhalia
sand dunes i amolofi
sandwich to 'sandwich'
sanitary towel i servi-eta
sardine i sarthela
Saturday to Savato
sauce i saltsa
saucepan i katsarola
saucer to piataki
sauna i saoona
sausage to lookaniko
say leo
scarf (*neck*) to kaskol; (*head*)
    to mandili
scenery to topio
school to sHolio
science i epistimi
scissors to psalithi
Scottish Skotsezoss
Scotland i Skotia
scream ksefonizo
screw i vitha
screwdriver to katsavithi
sea i THalassa
seafood ta THalassina
seagull o Glaross
seasick: I get seasick me
    piani i THalassa
seaside: at the seaside konda
    stin paralia
season i epoHi; in the high
    season stin THerini
    periotho
seat i THessi
seat belt i zoni asfaliass
seaweed ta fikia
second (*in time*) to
    thefterolepto
second-hand apo theftero Heri
secret mistikoss
see vlepo; see you
    tomorrow THa ta poome
    avrio

ENGLISH-GREEK

self-catering flat/cottage to aneksartito thiamerisma
self-service self-serviss
sell poolo
sellotape (R) to 'sellotape'
send stelno
sensible lo-yikoss
sensitive evesтнitoss
separate нoristoss
separately kseнorista
September o Septemvrioss
serious sovaross
serve eksipireto
service to serviss
service charge to filothorima
serviette i petseta
several arketi
sew ravo
sex to sex; (gender) to filo
sexist o falokratiss
sexy seksi
shade i skia; in the shade sti skia
shadow i skia
shampoo to sampoo-an
share (verb) mirazome
shark o karнariass
shave ksirizome
shaving brush to pinelo ya ksirisma
shaving foam o afross ksirismatoss
she afti (see grammar)
sheep to provato
sheet to sendoni
shell to kelifoss
shellfish ta ostraka
ship to plio
shirt to pookamisso
shock to sok
shock-absorber to amortisser
shocking eksofrenikoss
shoe laces ta korthonia

papootsion
shoe polish to verniki papootsion
shoe repairer o tsangariss
shoes ta papootsia
shop to maгazi
shopping ta psonia; go shopping pao ya psonia
shopping bag i tsanda
shopping centre to emboriko kendro
shore i akti
short (person) kondoss; (time) liгoss
shortcut o sindomoss thromoss
shorts to sorts
shortsighted miopass
shoulder o omoss
shout fonazo
show (verb) thiнno
shower to dooss; (rain) i bora
shutter (photo) to thiafraгma
shutters (window) ta padzooria
shy dropaloss
sick: I feel sick then nioтнo kala; I'm going to be sick eнo tassi pross emeto
side i plevra
sidelights ta нamila fota
sign (verb) ipoгrafo
silence i siopi
silk to metaksi
silver assimenioss
silver foil to aloominoнarto
similar paromioss
simple aploss
since (time) apo
sincere ilikriniss
sing traгootho
single (unmarried) elefтнeross

80

single room to mono thomatio
single ticket to aplo issitirio
sink o neroHitiss
sink (*go under*) vooliazo
sir kirie
sister i athelfi
sister-in-law (*brother's wife*) i nifi; (*wife's sister*) i kooniatha
sit down kaTHOme
size to me-yeTHOss
ski to ski
skid Glistro
skin to therma
skin cleanser kaTHaristiko thermatoss
skin-diving i katathississ
skinny kokaliariss
skirt i foosta
skull to kranio
sky o ooranoss
sleep kimame
sleeper i kooketa
sleeping bag to 'sleeping bag'
sleeping pill to ipnotiko Hapi
sleepy: I'm sleepy nistazo
slice i feta
slide (*phot*) to 'slide'
slim leptoss
slippers i pandofless
slippery Glisteross
slow arGoss
slowly siGa-siGa
small mikross
smell i mirothia
smell (*verb*) mirizo
smile to Hamo-yelo
smile (*verb*) Hamo-yelo
smoke o kapnoss
smoke (*verb*) kapnizo
smoking (*compartment*) kapnizondess

snack proHiro fa-yito
snail to salingari
snake to fithi
sneeze fternizome
snore roHalizo
snow to Hioni
so etsi; **so beautiful/big** tosso omorfoss/meGaloss
soap to sapooni
society i kinonia
socket i priza
socks i kaltsess
soft apaloss
soft drink to anapsiktiko
soft lenses i malaki faki
sole (*of shoe*) i sola
some meriki; **some wine/flour** liGo krassi/alevri
somebody kapioss
something kati
sometimes kamia fora
somewhere kapoo
son o yoss
song to traGoothi
son-in-law o Gambross
soon sindoma
sore: I've got a sore throat pona-i o lemoss moo
sorry lipame
so-so etsi ki etsi
soup i soopa
sour ksinoss
south notoss; **south of** notia apo
souvenir to enTHimio
spade to ftiari
Spain i Ispania
spanner to klithi
spare parts ta andalaktika
spare tyre i rezerva
spark plug to boozi
speak milo; **do you speak ...?** milate ...?

special delivery ekspress
speciality i spessialite
speed i taHitita
speed limit to orio taHititass
speedometer to konder
spend ksothevo
spice to baHariko
spider i araHni
spinach to spanaki
spoke i aktina
spoon to kootali
sport to spor
spot (*on skin*) i elia
**sprain: I've sprained my
  ankle** strabooliksa to pothi
  moo
spring (*season*) i aniksi; (*in
  seat etc*) to elatirio
square (*in town*) i platia
stain o lekess
stairs i skaless
stamp to Gramatossimo
stand adeHo; **I can't stand
  cheese** then m'aressi to tiri
star to asteri
state i politia
station o statHmoss
stationer's to Hartopolio
stay i thiamoni
stay (*remain, in hotel etc*) menc
steak i brizola
steal klevo
steep apotomoss
steering wheel to timoni
stepfather o patrioss
stepmother i mitria
steward o a-erossinothoss
stewardess i a-erossinothoss
still (*adverb*) akomi
sting tsimbo
stockings i na-ilon kaltsess
stomach to stomaHi
stomach ache o ponoss sto

stomaHi
stone i petra
stop i stassi
stop (*verb*) stamato; **stop!**
  stamata!
storm i tHi-ela
story i istoria
straight ahead issia brosta
strange (*odd*) paraksenoss
strawberry i fraoola
stream to rema
street o thromoss
stretch aplono
string to sHini
stroke (*attack*) to engefaliko
  epissothio
strong thinatoss
stuck frakarismenoss
student (*male*) o fititiss;
  (*female*) i fititria
stupid vlakass
suburbs ta pro-astia
success i epitiHia
suddenly ksafnika
sugar i zaHari
suit (*man's*) to koostoomi;
  (*woman's*) to ta-yer
suit: blue suits you soo pa-i
  to ble
suitcase i valitsa
summer to kalokeri
sun o ilioss
sunbathe kano iliotHerapia
sunburn to engavma apo ton
  ilio
Sunday i Kiriaki
sunglasses ta yalia ilioo
sunny ilioloostoss; **it's
  sunny** ehi liakatha
sunset i thissi too ilioo
sunshine i liakatha
sunstroke i iliassi
suntan to mavrisma apo ton ilio

ENGLISH-GREEK

suntan lotion/oil to lathi mavrismatoss
supermarket to 'supermarket'
sure siGooross
surname to epiTHeto
surprise i ekpliksi
surprising aprosmenoss
swallow katapino
sweat ithrono
sweater to poolover
sweet to Gliko
sweet (to taste) Glikoss
swim kolibo
swimming to kolibi; **go swimming** pao ya banio
swimming costume to ma-yo
swimming pool i pissina
swimming trunks to ma-yo
Swiss Elvetikoss
switch o thiakoptiss
switch off (light, television) klino; (engine) svino
switch on (light, television) aniGo; (engine) vazo bross
Switzerland i Elvetia
swollen prismenoss
synagogue i sinaGo-yi

T

table to trapezi
tablecloth to trapezomandilo
tablet i tableta
table tennis to ping-pong
tail i oora
take perno; **take away** (remove) perno; **to take away** (food) ya to spiti; **take off** (plane) apo-yionome

talcum powder i poothra talk
talk milo
tall psiloss
tampon to tabon
tank to depozito
tap i vrissi
tape (cassette) i kasseta
tart i pasta
taste yefsi
taste (try) thokimazo
taxi to taksi
tea to tsa-i
teach thithasko
teacher o thaskaloss
team i omatha
teapot i tsa-yera
tea towel i petseta tiss koozinass
teenager o neoss
telegram to tileGrafima
telephone to tilefono
telephone directory o tilefonikoss kataloGoss
television i tileorassi
temperature i THermokrassia
temple o naoss
tennis to teniss
tent (camping) i skini
terrible foveross
terrific ekseretikoss
than apo; **uglier than** pio asHimoss apo
thank efHaristo
thank you efHaristo
that (adjective) ekinoss, ekini, ekino; **that one** ekino; **I think that** nomizo oti
the o, i, to; (plural) i, i, ta (see grammar)
theatre to THe-atro
theft i klopi
their o/i/to ... tooss (see grammar)

theirs thiko tooss (see grammar)

them (object) tooss, tiss, ta; (after preposition) aftooss, aftess, afta (see grammar)

then tote

there eki; **there is/are** iparHi/iparHoon; **is/are there ...?** iparHi/iparHoon ...?

thermometer to THermometro

thermos flask to THermoss

these afti, aftess, afta

they afti, aftess, afta (see grammar)

thick paHiss

thief o kleftiss

thigh to booti

thin leptoss; (person) athinatoss

thing to praGma

think skeptome

thirsty: I'm thirsty thipso

this aftoss, afti, afto; **this one** afto etho

those ekini, ekiness, ekina

thread i klosti

throat o lemoss

throat pastilles pastili-ess lemoo

through thia messoo

throw riHno; **throw away** peto

thunder i vrodi

thunderstorm i THi-ela

Thursday i Pemdi

ticket to issitirio

ticket office i THiritha

tide i paliria

tie i Gravata

tight stenoss

tights to kalson

time o Hronoss; (occasion) i fora; **on time** stin ora too; **what time is it?** ti ora ine?

timetable to proGrama

tin opener to aniHtiri

tip to filothorima

tired koorasmenoss

tissues ta Hartomandila

to: I'm going to Crete/the harbour pao stin Kriti/sto limani

toast to tost

tobacco o kapnoss

today simera

toe to thaHtilo too pothioo

together mazi

toilet i too-aleta

toilet paper Harti iyiass

tomato i domata

tomorrow avrio

tongue i Glossa

tonight apopse

tonsillitis amiGthalititha

too poli; (also) epississ; **too much** para poli; **not too much** oHi para poli

tool to erGalio

tooth to thondi

toothache o ponothondoss

toothbrush i othondovoortsa

toothpaste i othondokrema

top: at the top stin korifi

torch o fakoss

touch angizo

tourist o tooristass

towel i petseta

tower o pirGoss

town i poli

town hall to thimarHio

toy to peHnithi

tracksuit i aTHlitiki forma

tradition i parathossi

traditional parathossiakoss

ENGLISH-GREEK

traffic i kikloforia
traffic jam i kikloforiaki
simforissi
traffic lights ta fanaria tiss
troHe-ass
traffic warden o
troHonomoss
trailer (*behind car*) i rimoolka
train to treno
trainers ta aTHlitika papootsia
translate metafrazo
travel taksithevo
travel agent's to taksithiotiko
Grafio
traveller's cheque i
taksithiotiki epita-yi
tray o thiskoss
tree to thendro
tremendous tromeross
trip to taksithi
trolley to 'trolley'
trousers to pandaloni
true aliTHinoss
try thokimazo; **try on**
thokimazo
T-shirt to bloozaki
Tuesday i Triti
tuna fish o tonoss
tunnel i siraga
turkey i Galopoola
Turkey i Toorkia
turn (*verb*) yirno
tweezers to tsimbithaki
twins i thithimi
typewriter i GrafomiHani
tyre to lastiHo

ugly aSHimoss

umbrella i obrela
uncle o THioss
under apo kato
underdone missopsimenoss
underground o ipo-yioss
underneath apo kato
underpants to slip
understand katalaveno
underwear ta essorooHa
unemployed anerGoss
unfortunately thistiHoss
United States Inomeness
Politi-ess
university to panepistimio
unpack aniGo tiss valitsess
unpleasant thissarestoss
until meHri
up: up there eki pano
upstairs pano
urgent epiGon
us mass (*see grammar*)
use Hrissimopio
useful Hrissimoss
usual siniTHismenoss
usually siniTHoss

vaccination o emvoliasmoss
vacuum cleaner i ilektriki
skoopa
vagina o kolposs
valid engiross
valley i kilatha
valve i valvitha
van to troHospito
vanilla i vanilia
vase to vazo
VD to afrothissio nossima
veal to mosHari

85

vegetables ta laнanika
vegetarian o нortofaɢoss
vehicle to oнima
very poli; **very much** para poli
vet o ktiniatross
video to 'video'
view i тнe-a
villa i vila
village to нorio
vinegar to ksithi
vineyard to abeli
visa i viza
visit i episkepsi
visit (verb) episkeptome
vitamins i vitaminess
voice i foni

waist i messi
wait perimeno; **wait for me!** perimene me!
waiter o servitoross
waiting room i eтнoossa anamoniss
waitress i servitora
wake up ksipno
Wales i Ooalia
walk o peripatoss; **go for a walk** pao peripato
walk (verb) perpato
walkman (R) to 'walkman'
wall o tiнoss
wallet to portofoli
want тнelo; **I want** тнelo; **do you want . . .?** тнelete . . .?
war o polemoss

warm zestoss; **it's warm** kani zesti
wash pleno; (oneself) plenome
washbasin o niptirass
washing i booɢatha; **do the washing** vazo booɢatha
washing machine to plindirio
washing powder i skoni plindirioo
washing-up to plissimo ton piaton; **do the washing-up** pleno ta piata
washing-up liquid to sapooni piaton
wasp i sfinga
watch (for time) to rolo-i
watch (verb) vlepo
water to nero
waterfall o kataraktiss
waterskiing to тнalasso ski
wave (in sea) to kima
way: this way (like this) etsi; **can you tell me the way to the . . .?** borite na moo pite poss pane sto . . .?
we emiss (see grammar)
weak athinatoss
weather o keross; **the weather's good** eнi kalo kero
weather forecast to meteorolo-yiko theltio
wedding o ɢamoss
Wednesday i Tetarti
week i evthomatha
weekend to Savatokiriako
weight to vaross
welcome! kaloss ilтнate!
well: he's well/he's not well ine kala/then ine kala
well (adverb) kala

ENGLISH-GREEK

well done (*meat*)
  kalopsimenoss
wellingtons i Galotsess
Welsh Ooaloss
west i thissi; **west of** thitika
  apo
wet iGross
what? ti?; **what's this?** ti ine
  afto?
wheel i rotha
wheelchair i anapiriki
  poliтнrona
when? pote?
when otan
where? poo?
which? pio?
while eno
whipped cream sadiyi
whisky to 'whisky'
white aspross
who? pioss?
whole oloklıross
whooping cough o kokitiss
whose? too opioo; **whose is
  this?** pianoo ine afto?
why? yiati?
wide platiss
widow i Hira
widower o Hiross
wife i yineka
wild aGrioss
win kerthizo
wind o anemoss
window to paraтнiro
windscreen to parbriz
windscreen wiper o
  ialokaтнaristirass
wine to krassi;
  red/white/rosé wine
  kokino/aspro/roze krassi
wine list o kataloGoss ton
  krassion
wing to ftero

winter o Himonass
wire to sirma
wish: best wishes poless
  efнess
with me
without Horiss
witness o martirass
woman i yineka
wonderful тнavmassioss
wood to ksilo
wool to mali
word i leksi
work i thoolia
work (*verb*) erGazome; **it's
  not working** then thoolevi
world o kosmoss
worry i stenoнoria
worry about anisiнo ya
worry beads to kombolo-i
worse Hiroteross
worst o Hiroteross
wound i pliyi
wrap tiliGo
wrapping paper to Harti
  peritiliGmatoss
wrench to klithi
wrist o karposs
write Grafo
writing paper to Harti
  aliloGrafiass
wrong laтнoss

X-ray i aktinoGrafia

87

yacht to yot
year o Hronoss
yellow kitrinoss
yes ne
yesterday H-THess
yet: not yet oHi akomi
yoghurt to ya-oorti
you (*familiar*) essi; (*plural or polite*) essiss; (*object*) se/sass
young neoss; **young people** i ne-i
your (*familiar*) o/i/to ... soo; (*plural or polite*) o/i/to ... sass (*see grammar*)
yours (*familiar*) thiko soo; (*plural or polite*) thiko sass (*see grammar*)
youth hostel o ksenonass neon
Yugoslavia i Yoogoslavia

zero mithen
zip to fermoo-ar
zoo o zo-oloyikoss kiposs

Αα

αγαπώ love
αγάπη (η) love
αγαπημένος favourite
αγαπητός dear
αγγίζω touch
Αγγλία (η) England
Αγγλίδα (η) Englishwoman
Αγγλικός English; στα
  Αγγλικά in English
Άγγλος (ο) Englishman
αγγούρι (το) cucumber
αγελάδα (η) cow
αγενής rude
άγκυρα (η) anchor
αγκώνας (ο) elbow
αγορά (η) market
αγοράζω buy
αγόρι (το) boy
άγριος wild
αγρόκτημα (το) farm
αγρότης (ο) farmer
αγώνας (ο) fight; game
άδεια (η) licence;
  permission
άδεια οδηγήσεως (η) driving
  licence
άδειος empty
αδελφή (η) sister
αδελφός (ο) brother
αδύνατος impossible
αδύνατος weak
αέρας (ο) air; choke

αεριούχο fizzy
αεροδρόμιο (το) airport
αεροπλάνο (το) plane
αεροπορική εταιρεία (η)
  airline
αεροπορικώς by air; airmail
αεροσυνοδός (η) air hostess
αεροσυνοδός (ο) steward
Αθήνα (η) Athens
αθλητής (ο) athlete
αθλητικά παπούτσια (τα)
  trainers
αθλητική φορμα (η) tracksuit
αθώος innocent
Αιγαίο (το) Aegean
αίθουσα αναμονής (η)
  waiting room
αίμα (το) blood
αιμορραγώ bleed
αιμορροΐδες (οι) piles
αισθάνομαι feel
αισιόδοξος optimistic
αίτηση (η) application (form)
αιτία (η) cause
αιώνας (ο) century
ακολουθώ follow
ακόμα, ακόμη still, yet;
  even; ακόμα κι άν even if
ακουστικά (τα) hearing aid
ακούω hear
ακριβός expensive
άκρη (η) edge
ακροατήριο (το) audience
ακτή (η) coast; shore
ακτινογραφία (η) X-ray
ακυρώνω cancel

Β Γ Δ Ζ Η Θ Λ Μ Ν Ξ Π Ρ Σ Υ Φ Χ Ψ Ω ΑΙ ΑΥ ΕΙ ΕΥ ΟΙ ΟΥ ΜΠ ΝΤ
β γ δ ζ η θ λ μ ν ξ π ρ σ υ φ χ ψ ω αι αυ ει ευ οι ου μπ ντ
v y th z i TH l m n x p r s i f H ps o e af i e f i oo b d

αλάτι (το) salt
Αλβανία (η) Albania
αλεύρι (το) flour
αληθινός true
αλκοόλ (το) alcohol
αλλά but
αλλάζω change; αλλάζω
  ρούχα change (clothes)
αλλεργία (η) allergy
αλλεργία στη γύρη (η) ·hay
  fever
αλλεργικός σε allergic to
άλλος, άλλη, άλλο other;
  else; όχι άλλο no more;
  άλλος ένας, άλλη μία, άλλο
  ένα another
αλλού elsewhere
αλμυρός salty
άλογο (το) horse
αλοιφή (η) ointment
αλουμινόχαρτο (το) silver
  foil
αλτ! stop!
αλυσίδα (η) chain
αμάξι (το) car
Αμερικανίδα (η) American
  (woman)
Αμερικανικός American
Αμερικανός (ο) American
  (man)
Αμερική (η) America
αμέσως immediately
άμμος (η) sand
αμορτισέρ (το) shock-
  absorber
αμπέλι (το) vineyard
αμυγδαλίτιδα (η) tonsillitis
αν if
αν και although
ανάβω light (verb)
αναγκαίο necessary

ανάγκη (η) need
αναγνωρίζω recognize
αναμειγνύω mix
ανάμεσα among
ανανάς (ο) pineapple
αναπαύομαι take a rest
ανάπαυση (η) rest
αναπαυτικός comfortable
αναπηρική πολυθρόνα (η)
  wheelchair; pushchair
ανάπηρος disabled
αναπνέω breathe
αναποδογυρίζω knock over
αναπτήρας (ο) lighter
αναπτύσσω develop
ανατολή (η) east
ανατολικά (από) east (of)
αναχώρηση (η) departure
αναψυκτικό (το) soft drink
άνδρας (ο) man
ανδρών gents
ανεβαίνω get in (car); get
  up; go up
ανεξάρτητο διαμέρισμα (το)
  self-catering flat/cottage
ανεμιστήρας (ο) fan
άνεμος (ο) wind
ανεξάρτητος independent
άνεργος unemployed
ανήκω belong
ανησυχώ για worry about
ανηψιά (η) niece
ανηψιός (ο) nephew
ανθοπώλης (ο) florist
άνθρωποι (οι) people
ανοίγω open; switch on
ανοικτός open; light
  (colour); on (light)
άνοιξη (η) spring (season)
ανοιχτήρι (το) corkscrew;
  tin opener

ανοιχτό μπλε light blue
ανταλλακτικά (τα) spares
ανταλλάσω exchange
αντέχω stand
αντιβιοτικό (το) antibiotic
αντιισταμινικό φάρμακο
  (το) antihistamine
αντίκα antique
αντίο goodbye
αντιπαθητικός obnoxious
αντιπρόσωπος (ο) agent
αντισηπτικό (το) antiseptic
αντισυλληπτικό (το)
  contraceptive pill
αντιψυκτικό (το) antifreeze
αντλία (η) pump
άξονας (ο) axle
απαγορέυεται it is prohibited
απαγορευμένος forbidden
απαίσιος appalling
απαιτώ demand
απαλός soft
απαντώ answer
απάντηση (η) answer
απέναντι opposite
απένταρος broke
απεριτίφ (το) aperitif
απίθανος incredible
απλό εισιτήριο (το) single
  ticket
απλός simple
απλώνω stretch
από from; since (time);
  than; από κάτω below,
  under; από πάνω over (above)
αποβιβάζομαι land
απογειώνομαι take off (plane)
απόγευμα (το) afternoon
απογοητευμένος
  disappointed
απόδειξη (η) receipt
απολυμαντικό (το)
  disinfectant

αποσκευές (οι) luggage
αποσμητικό (το) deodorant
απόσταση (η) distance
απότομος steep
αποφασίζω decide
απόψε tonight
Απρίλιος (ο) April
απρόσμενος surprising
αράχνη (η) spider
αργά late
αργώ arrive late; be slow
αργίες (οι) holidays (public)
αργός slow
αρέσω: μου αρέσει . . . I
  like . . .
αριθμός (ο) number
αριστερά left; στα
  αριστερά on the left
αριστερόχειρας left-handed
αρκετά enough; quite
αρκετοί several
αρνητικό (το) negative
αρνί (το) lamb
αρουραίος (ο) rat
αρραβωνιασμένος engaged
αρραβωνιαστικός (ο) fiancé
αρραβωνιαστικιά (η) fiancée
αρρενωπός manly; macho
αρρώστια (η) disease
άρρωστος ill
αρχαιολογία (η) archaeology
αρχαίος ancient
αρχαιότητες (οι) ruins
αρχάριος (ο) beginner
αρχή (η) beginning
αρχίζω begin
άρωμα (το) perfume
ασανσέρ (το) lift
ασετόν (το) nail polish
  remover
ασημένιος silver
ασθενοφόρο (το) ambulance
άσθμα (το) asthma

ΒΓΔΖΗΘ ΛΜΝΞ ΠΡΣ ΥΦΧ ΨΩ ΑΙ ΑΥ ΕΙ ΕΥ ΟΙ ΟΥ ΜΠ ΝΤ
β γ δ ζ η θ λ μ ν ξ π ρ σ υ φ χ ψ ω αι αυ ει ευ οι ου μπ ντ
v y th z i TH l m n x p r s i f H ps o e af i ef i oo b d

ασπιρίνη (η) aspirin
άσπρος white
αστακός (ο) lobster
άστατος changeable
αστείο (το) joke
αστείος funny, amusing
αστέρι (το) star
αστυνομία (η) police
αστράγαλος (ο) ankle
αστυνομικό τμήμα (το)
 police station
αστυφύλακας (ο) policeman
ασφάλεια (η) fuse;
 insurance
ασφαλής safe
άσχημα badly
άσχημος ugly
ατζέντα (η) address book;
 agenda
άτομο (το) person
αυγό (το) egg; αυγό
 βραστό boiled egg; αυγό
 σφιχτό hard-boiled egg
Αύγουστος (ο) August
αυθεντικός genuine
αϋπνία (η) insomnia
αύριο tomorrow
Αυστραλέζα (η) Australian
 (woman)
Αυστραλέζικος Australian
Αυστραλία (η) Australia
Αυστραλός (ο) Australian
 (man)
Αυστρία (η) Austria
Αυστριακός Austrian
AUTAN (R) (το) insect
 repellent
αυτή she
αυτί (το) ear
αυτό it; this; αυτό εδώ
 this one; αυτό που what

αυτοί, αυτές, αυτά these;
 they
αυτοκίνητο (το) car
αυτόματος automatic
αυτός he
αυτός, αυτή, αυτό this (one)
αυτός ο ίδιος himself
αυτούς, αυτές, αυτά them
αφεντικό (το) boss
αφήνω leave
άφιξη (η) arrival
αφίσα (η) poster
αφορολόγητα (τα) duty-free
αφροδίσιο νόσημα (το) VD
αφρός (ο) surf
αφρός ξυρίσματος (ο)
 shaving foam
αχθοφόρος (ο) doorman
αχλάδι (το) pear

Ββ

βαγόνι (το) carriage (train)
βάζο (το) vase
βάζω put; βάζω μπρος
 switch on (engine)
βάθος: στο βάθος in the
 background, at the bottom
βαθύς deep
βαλβίδα (η) valve
βαλίτσα (η) bag, suitcase;
 φτιάχνω/ανοίγω τις
 βαλίτσες pack/unpack
βαμβακερό (το) cotton
βαμβάκι (το) cotton wool
βανίλια (η) vanilla
βαρετός boring
βαριέμαι I'm bored; έχω
 βαρεθεί I'm fed up

92

βάρκα με μηχανή (η) motorboat
βάρκα με κουπιά (η) rowing boat
βάρος (το) weight
βαρύς heavy; rich (food)
βασιλιάς (ο) king
βασίλισσα (η) queen
βατόμουρο (το) blackberry
βάφω paint (walls)
βγαίνω go out
βέβαια of course
Βελγικός Belgian
Βέλγιο (το) Belgium
βελόνα (η) needle
βελτιώνω improve
βενζινάδικο (το) petrol station
βενζίνη (η) petrol
βεντιλατέρ (το) fan belt
βερίκοκο (το) apricot
βερνίκι παπουτσιών (το) shoe polish
βήχας (ο) cough
βήχω cough
βιάζομαι hurry; βιάσου! hurry up!
βιασμός (ο) rape
βιβλίο (το) book
βιβλίο διαλόγων (το) phrase book
βιβλιοθήκη (η) library
βιβλιοπωλείο (το) bookshop
βίδα (η) screw
βίζα (η) visa
βίλλα (η) villa
βίντεο (το) video
βιομηχανία (η) industry
βιταμίνες (οι) vitamins
βλάβη (η) breakdown (car)
βλάκας (ο) idiot
βλάκας stupid
βλέπω see

βοήθεια (η) help
βοηθώ help
βόμβα (η) bomb
βορράς (ο) north
βόρεια (από) north (of)
Βόρειος Ιρλανδία (η) Northern Ireland
βότανα (τα) herbs
Βουλγαρία (η) Bulgaria
βουλιάζω sink
βουνό (το) mountain
βούρτσα (η) brush
βουτώ dive
βούτυρο (το) butter
βράδυ (το) evening
βραδιά (η) evening
βράζω boil
βραχιόλι (το) bracelet
βράχος (ο) rock
Βρεταννία (η) Britain
Βρεταννίδα (η) Briton (woman)
Βρεταννικός British
Βρεταννός (ο) Briton (man)
βρέχει it's raining
βρίσκω find
βροντή (η) thunder
βροχή (η) rain
βρύση (η) tap
βρώμικος dirty
βυζαίνω breastfeed
βυθός (ο) bottom (of sea)

Γγ

γάιδαρος (ο) donkey
γάλα (το) milk
γαλάκτωμα καθαρισμού (το) cleansing cream
Γαλλία (η) France
Γαλλικός French

ΒΓΔΖΗΘ ΛΜΝΞΠΡΣ ΥΦΧΨΩ ΑΙ ΑΥ ΕΙ ΕΥ ΟΙ ΟΥ ΜΠ ΝΤ
β γ δ ζ η θ λ μ ν ξ π ρ σ υ φ χ ψ ω αι αυ ει ευ οι ου μπ ντ
v y th z i TH l m n x p r s i f H ps o e af i ef i oo b d

γαλοπούλα (η) turkey
γαλότσες (οι) wellingtons
γάμος (ο) wedding
γαμπρός (ο) bridegroom;
  son-in-law; brother-in-law
γάντια (τα) gloves
γαρίδα (η) prawn
γάτα (η) cat
γειά σου hello; bless you!;
  cheers
γείτονας (ο) neighbour
γελοίο ridiculous
γελώ laugh
γεμάτος full
γεμίζω fill
γενέθλια (τα) birthday
γένια (τα) beard
γενναίος brave
γεννήθηκα το ... I was born
  in ...
Γερμανία (η) Germany
Γερμανικός German
γέρος old (person)
γεύμα (το) lunch; meal
γεύση (η) flavour; taste
γέφυρα (η) bridge
για for
γιαγιά (η) grandmother
γιακάς (ο) collar
γιαούρτι (το) yoghurt
γιατί; why?
γιατρός (ο) doctor
γίνομαι become
γιός (ο) son
Γιουγκοσλαβία η Yugoslavia
γιώτ (το) yacht
γκάζι (το) gas; accelerator
γκαρνταρόμπα (η) cloakroom
  (coats)
γκολφ (το) golf
γκρέιπφρουτ (το) grapefruit

γκρίζος grey
γκρουπ (το) group
γλάρος (ο) seagull
γλιφιτζούρι (το) lollipop
γλύκισμα (το) dessert
γλυκό (το) sweet
γλυκός sweet (to taste)
γλυστερός slippery
γλυστρώ skid
γλώσσα (η) language;
  tongue
γνωρίζω know
γόνατο (το) knee
γονείς (οι) parents
γουίντσερφ (το) sailboard
γουόκμαν (το) walkman (R)
γουρούνι (το) pig
γοφός (ο) hip
γραβάτα (η) tie
γράμμα (το) letter
γράμματα (τα) post (mail)
γραμματική (η) grammar
γραμματοκιβώτιο (το)
  letterbox
γραμματόσημο (το) stamp
γρασίδι (το) lawn
γραφείο (το) office
γραφείο απωλεσθέντων (το)
  lost property office
γραφομηχανή (η) typewriter
γράφω write
γρήγορα quick; quickly
γρήγορος fast
γρίπη (η) flu
γρύλλος (ο) jack
γυαλί (το) glass (substance)
γυαλιά (τα) glasses
γυαλιά ηλίου (τα) sunglasses
γυμνασμένος fit (healthy)
γυμνός naked
γυναίκα (η) wife; woman

γυρνώ turn (*verb*)
γυρνώ πίσω arrive back,
    return; take back; γυρνώ
    σπίτι go home
γωνία (η) corner

Δδ

δακτυλίδι (το) ring (*on finger*)
δαμάσκηνο (το) plum
δανείζομαι borrow
δανείζω lend
δάσκαλος (ο) instructor;
    teacher
δάσος (το) forest
δάχτυλο (το) finger
δάχτυλο του ποδιού (το) toe
ΔΕΗ National Electricity
    Board
δείκτης (ο) gauge; index
    finger
δείπνο (το) dinner
δείχνω show
δεκαπενθήμερο (το)
    fortnight
Δεκέμβριος (ο) December
δέμα (το) parcel
δεν not
δένδρο (το) tree
δεξιά right (*side*)
δεξίωση reception (*party*)
δέρμα leather; skin
δεσποινίδα (η) Miss
Δευτέρα (η) Monday
δεύτερη θέση second class
δευτερόλεπτο (το) second
δεύτερος second; από
    δεύτερο χέρι second-hand
δέχομαι accept; receive
δηλητηρίαση (η) poisoning
δηλητήριο (το) poison

δημαρχείο (το) town hall
δημόσιος public
δημοτική μουσική (η) folk
    music
διαβάζω read
διάβαση πεζών (η)
    pedestrian crossing
διαβατήριο (το) passport
διαβητικός (ο) diabetic
διάδρομος (ο) corridor
διάθεση (η) mood
δίαιτα (η) diet
διακλάδωση (η) fork (*in road*)
διακοπές (οι) holiday
διακοπή (η) interruption;
    power cut
διακόπτης (ο) switch
διακόπτω interrupt
διαλέγω choose
διάλεκτος (η) dialect
διαμάντι (το) diamond
Διαμαρτυρόμενος (ο)
    Protestant
διαμέρισμα (το) apartment;
    flat
διά μέσου through
διαμονή (η)
    accommodation; stay
διάρκεια (η) duration
διαρροή (η) leak
διάρροια (η) diarrhoea
διάσημος famous
διασκέδαση: καλή
    διασκέδαση! have fun!
διασταύρωση (η) junction
διασχίζω go through
διαφημιστικό (το) leaflet
διαφορετικά otherwise
διαφορετικός different
διάφραγμα (το) shutter
διαχειριστής (ο) manager
διδάσκω teach
δίδυμοι (οι) twins

ΒΓΔΖΗΘ ΛΜΝΞΠΡΣΥΦΧΨΩ ΑΙ ΑΥ ΕΙ ΕΥ ΟΙ ΟΥ ΜΠ ΝΤ
β γ δ ζ η θ λ μ ν ξ π ρ σ υ φ χ ψ ω αι αυ ει ευ οι ου μπ ντ
v y th z i TH l m n x p r s i f H ps o e af i e f i oo b d

διεύθυνση (η) address
δίκαιος fair
δικηγόρος (ο) lawyer
δικός μου mine
δικός μας ours
δικός σου yours
δικός σας yours
δικός της hers
δικός του his, its
δικός τους theirs
δίνω give
διορθώνω mend
δίπλα από next to
διπλό double
διπλό δωμάτιο (το) double
 room
δισκάδικο (το) record shop
δίσκος (ο) record; tray
διψώ I'm thirsty
δοκιμάζω taste; try; try on
δόντι (το) tooth
δουλειά (η) job; work
δουλεύω work; δεν
 δουλεύει it's not working
δουλειές (οι) business
δρόμος (ο) road; street
δροσερός cool
δυνατός loud; possible;
 strong
δυσάρεστος unpleasant
δύση του ήλιου (η) sunset
δυσκοιλία (η) constipation
δύσκολος difficult
δυσπεψία (η) indigestion
δυστύχημα (το) accident
δυστυχώς unfortunately
δυτικός western
δυτικά (από) west (of)
δωμάτιο (το) room
δωρεάν free (of charge)
δώρο (το) present

Εε

EAP Greek Left Union
EAΣ Athens Public
 Transport Corporation
εβδομάδα (η) week; την
 εβδομάδα per week
Εβραίος Jewish
έγγραφο (το) document
εγγύηση (η) guarantee
εγκαίρως on time
έγκαυμα από τον ήλιο (το)
 sunburn
εγκεφαλικό επεισόδιο (το)
 stroke (attack)
έγκυος pregnant
έγκυρος valid
εγχείρηση (η) operation
έγχρωμο φιλμ (το) colour
 film
εγώ I
εδώ here
έθιμο (το) custom
εθνική οδός (η) motorway
εθνικότητα (η) nationality
ειδικώς especially
ειλικρινής sincere
είμαι I am
είναι he/she/it/ is
εισιτήριο (το) ticket
εισιτήριο με επιστροφή
 return ticket
είσοδος (η) entrance
εκατό one hundred; τοις
 εκατό per cent
εκεί there, over there
εκείνο that one
εκείνοι, εκείνες, εκείνα
 those

εκείνος, εκείνη, εκείνο that
έκθεση (η) exhibition
εκκλησία (η) church
έκπληξη (η) surprise
εκπληκτικός surprising
εκπτώσεις (οι) sales
έκτατη ανάγκη (η)
  emergency
εκτός except
ελαιόλαδο (το) olive oil
ελαστικός elastic
ελατήριο (το) spring
ελαττωματικός faulty
ελαφρός light (not heavy)
Ελβετία (η) Switzerland
Ελβετικός Swiss
ελεγκτής (ο) inspector (bus)
ελεύθερος free; single
  (unmarried)
ελιά (η) olive; spot (on skin)
ελικόπτερο (το) helicopter
ελκυστικός attractive
Ελλάδα (η) Greece
Έλληνας (ο) Greek (man)
Ελληνίδα (η) Greek (woman)
Ελληνικά (τα) Greek
  (language)
Ελληνικός Greek
ελπίζω hope
εμβόλιο (το) vaccine
εμβολιασμός (ο) vaccination
εμείς we
εμένα me
εμετός (ο) vomit
εμπορικό κέντρο (το)
  shopping centre
εναντίον against
ένας, μια, ένα a; one
ενδιαφέρον interesting
ένεση (η) injection
ενήλικος (ο) adult
ενθύμιο (το) souvenir
εννοώ mean (verb)

ενοικιάζεται for hire; to
  rent
ενοικίαση αυτοκινήτων (η)
  car rental
ενοίκιο (το) rent
ενοχλητικός annoying
ενοχλώ disturb
εντάξει that's all right; OK
έντομο (το) insect
έντυπα printed matter
ενώ while
εξαιρετικός terrific
εξ αιτίας because of
εξαρτάται it depends
εξάτμιση (η) exhaust
εξαφανίζομαι disappear
εξηγώ explain
έξοδος (η) exit; gate (airport)
έξοδος κινδύνου (η)
  emergency exit
εξοχή (η) countryside
έξοχος excellent
εξπρές express
εξυπηρετώ serve
έξυπνος clever, intelligent
έξω outside; έξω! get out!
εξωτερικός external; στο
  εξωτερικό abroad
εξωφρενικός shocking
EOK European Economic
  Community
EOT National Tourism
  Agency
επαληθεύω verify
επαναλαμβάνω repeat
επείγον urgent
επειδή because
επέκταση (η) extension lead
επέτειος (η) anniversary
επιβάτης (ο) passenger
επιβεβαιώνω confirm
επίδεσμος (ο) bandage
επίθεση (η) attack

Β Γ Δ Ζ Η Θ Λ Μ Ν Ξ Π Ρ Σ Υ Φ Χ Ψ Ω ΑΙ ΑΥ ΕΙ ΕΥ ΟΙ ΟΥ ΜΠ ΝΤ
β γ δ ζ η θ λ μ ν ξ π ρ σ υ φ χ ψ ω αι αυ ει ευ οι ου μπ ντ
v y th z i TH l m n x p r s i f H ps o e af i ef i oo b d

επιθετικός aggressive
επίθετο (το) surname
επικίνδυνος dangerous
επιληπτικός (ο) epileptic
επίπεδος flat
έπιπλα (τα) furniture
επίσης too, also; και εγώ
   επίσης me too
επισκέπτομαι visit
επισκευή (η) repair
επίσκεψη (η) visit
επιστήμη (η) science
επιστρέφω give back; arrive
   back
επιταγή (η) cheque
επιτέλους at last
επίτηδες deliberately
επιτρέπω let (allow)
επιτρέπεται it is permitted
επιτυχία (η) success
επόμενος (ο) next
εποχή (η) season
εργάζομαι work
εργαλείο (το) tool
εργένης (ο) bachelor
εργοστάσιο (το) factory
ερυθρά (η) German measles
έρχομαι come; έρχομαι σε
   επαφή contact
έρωτας (ο) love; κάνω
   έρωτα make love; είμαι
   ερωτευμένος I am in love
ερώτηση (η) question
εστιατόριο (το) restaurant
εσείς you (plural, polite)
εσένα you (after prepositions)
εσύ you (familiar)
ΕΣΥ National Health
   Service
εσώρουχα (τα) underwear
εταιρεία (η) company

ετικέτα (η) label
ετοιμάζω prepare
έτοιμος ready
έτσι so; like this
έτσι κι έτσι so-so
ευαίσθητος sensitive
ευγενικός kind; polite
ευγνώμων grateful
ΕΥΔΑΠ Athens Water
   Board
εύκολος easy
Ευρωπαϊκός European
Ευρώπη (η) Europe
ευτυχισμένος happy;
   ευτυχισμένος ο καινούργιος
   χρόνος happy New Year!
ευτυχώς fortunately
ευχαριστημένος pleased
ευχάριστος pleasant
ευχαριστώ thank you
εφημερίδα (η) newspaper
εφημεριδοπώλης (ο)
   newsagent
εφιάλτης (ο) nightmare
έχω have; έχετε ποτέ ...;
   have you ever ...?;
   έχετε/έχεις ...; have you
   got ...?

ζακέτα (η) cardigan
ζαμπόν (το) ham
ζάχαρη (η) sugar
ζαχαροπλαστείο (το) cake
   shop
ζέστη (η) heat; κάνει ζέστη
   it's warm
ζεστός hot; warm

ζευγάρι (το) pair
ζηλιάρης jealous
ζημιά (η) damage
ζητώ συγνώμη apologize
ζω live
ζωγραφίζω paint (pictures)
ζωγραφική (η) painting
ζωή (η) life
ζώνη (η) belt
ζώνη ασφαλείας (η) seat belt
ζωντανός alive
ζώο (το) animal
ζωολογικός κήπος (ο) zoo

η the
ή or; ή...ή... either...
  or...
ήδη already
ηλεκτρική σκούπα (η)
  vacuum cleaner
ηλεκτρικό ρεύμα (το)
  electricity
ηλεκτρικός electric
ηλίαση (η) sunstroke
ηλικία (η) age
ηλιοθεραπεία (η)
  sunbathing
ηλιόλουστος sunny
ήλιος (ο) sun
ημέρα (η) day
ημερολόγιο (το) calendar
ημερολόγιο (το) diary
ημερομηνία (η) date
ημιδιατροφή (η) half board
Ηνωμένες Πολιτείες (οι)
  United States
ΗΠΑ USA
ηρεμώ calm down
ήσυχος quiet

θάλασσα (η) sea
θαλασσινά (τα) seafood
θαλάσσιο σκι (το)
  waterskiing
θάνατος (ο) death
θαυμάσιος wonderful
θέα (η) view
θεά (η) goddess
θεατρικό έργο (το) play
θέατρο (το) theatre
θεία (η) aunt
θείος (ο) uncle
θέλω want; θέλετε...; do
  you want...?; θα ήθελα I
  would like
θεός (ο) God
θέρμανση (η) heating
θερμοκρασία (η)
  temperature
θερμόμετρο (το)
  thermometer
θερμός (το) thermos flask
θέση (η) seat
θλιμμένος depressed; sad
θορυβώδης noisy
θρησκεία (η) religion
θύελλα (η) storm;
  thunderstorm
θυμάμαι remember
θυμωμένος angry
θυρωρός (ο) doorman;
  caretaker; porter (hotel)

Ιανουάριος (ο) January
ιδέα (η) idea

Β Γ Δ Ζ Η Θ Λ Μ Ν Ξ Π Ρ Σ Υ Φ Χ Ψ Ω ΑΙ ΑΥ ΕΙ ΕΥ ΟΙ ΟΥ ΜΠ ΝΤ
β γ δ ζ η θ λ μ ν ξ π ρ σ υ φ χ ψ ω αι αυ ει ευ οι ου μπ ντ
v y th z i TH l m n x p r s i f H ps o e af i efi oo b d

ιδιοκτήτης (ο) owner
ίδιος same; εγώ ο ίδιος
  myself
ιδιωτικός private
ιδρώνω sweat
ιλαρά (η) measles
Ιούλιος (ο) July
Ιούνιος (ο) June
ιππασία (η) horse riding
Ιρλανδέζα (η) Irishwoman
Ιρλανδία (η) Ireland
Ιρλανδικός Irish
Ιρλανδός (ο) Irishman
ίσια straight; ίσια μπροστά
  straight ahead
ισόγειο (το) ground floor
Ισπανία (η) Spain
Ισπανικός Spanish
ιστιοπλοΐα (η) sailing
ιστιοπλοϊκό σκάφος (το)
  sailing boat
ιστορία (η) story; history
ίσως maybe
Ιταλία Italy
Ιταλικός Italian

Κ κ

καβούρι (το) crab
καθαρίζω clean
καθαριστήριο (το) laundry
καθαριστικό δέρματος (το)
  skin cleanser
καθαρός clean
καθαρτικό (το) laxative
κάθε every; κάθε τί
  everything
καθένας, καθεμία, καθένα each
καθηγητής (ο) teacher

καθολικός Catholic
καθόλου not at all, none; any
κάθομαι sit down
καθρέφτης (ο) mirror
καθρέφτης αυτοκινήτου (ο)
  rearview mirror
καθυστέρηση (η) delay
καθυστερώ delay; be late
και and
καινούργιος brand-new
και οι δύο both of them
καιρός (ο) weather
καίω burn
κακός bad
καλά well; καλά! good!;
  όλα καλά that'll do nicely
καλάθι (το) basket
καλημέρα good morning
καληνύχτα good night
καλησπέρα good evening
καλλιτέχνης (ο) artist
καλλυντικά (τα) cosmetics
καλοκαίρι (το) summer
καλοκαιρινές διακοπές (οι)
  summer holidays
καλοριφέρ (το) radiator
καλός good; kind
καλοψημένος well done
  (*meat*)
καλσόν (το) tights
κάλτσες (οι) socks
καλύτερος better;
  καλύτερος από better than
καλύτερος (ο) the best
καλώς ήλθατε! welcome!
καμαριέρα (η) chambermaid
καμμιά φορά sometimes
καμπάνα (η) bell
καμπίνα (η) cabin (*ship*)
κάμπινγκ (το) campsite
Καναδάς (ο) Canada

Καναδή (η) Canadian (woman)

Καναδικός Canadian

Καναδός (o) Canadian (man)

κανάτα (η) jug

κάνει (κρύο) it is (cold)

κανένας nobody

κανό (το) canoe

καντράν του αυτοκινήτου (το) dashboard

κάνω do; make

καπάκι (το) lid

καπαρντίνα (η) raincoat

καπάκι (το) cap (of bottle)

καπέλο (το) hat, cap

καπετάνιος (o) captain (ship)

καπνίζοντες smoking

καπνίζω smoke

καπνός (o) smoke; tobacco

καπό (το) bonnet (car)

κάποιος somebody

κάπου somewhere

καραβίδα (η) crayfish

καρδιά (η) heart

καρδιακή προσβολή (η) heart attack

καρέκλα (η) chair

καρμπιρατέρ (το) carburettor

καρνέ επιταγών (το) cheque book

καρότο (το) carrot

καροτσάκι (το) pram

καρπός (o) wrist

κάρτα (η) business card; postcard

κάρτα επιβιβάσεως (η) boarding pass

κάρτα επιταγών (η) cheque card

καρτποστάλ (η) postcard

καρύδι (το) nut (to eat)

καρφί (το) nail (in wall)

καρφίτσα (η) pin; brooch

καρχαρίας (o) shark

κασέτα (η) cassette

κασετόφωνο (το) cassette player

κασκόλ (το) scarf (neck)

κασέτα (η) tape (cassette)

κάστανο (το) chestnut

καστόρ suede

κάστρο (το) castle

κατα τη διάρκεια while, during

κάταγμα (το) fracture

καταδύσεις (οι) skin-diving

καταλαβαίνω understand

κατάλογος (o) list; menu

κατάλογος κρασιών (o) wine list

καταπίνω swallow

καταρράκτης (o) waterfall

κατασκήνωση (η) camping

κατάστημα αφορολογήτων (το) duty-free shop

καταστροφή (η) disaster

κατάστρωμα (το) deck

καταψύκτης (o) freezer

κατάψυξη (η) freezer compartment

κατεβαίνω get off; go down

κατειλημμένος engaged; occupied

κατευθείαν direct

κατεύθυνση (η) direction

κατεψυγμένος frozen (food)

κάτι something; κάτι άλλο something else

κατσαβίδι (το) screwdriver

κατσαρίδα (η) cockroach

κατσαρόλα (η) saucepan

κατσίκα (η) goat

κάτω down; downstairs; κάτω από under; εκεί κάτω down there

καυτερός spicy, hot

B Γ Δ Ζ Η Θ Λ Μ Ν Ξ Π Ρ Σ Υ Φ Χ Ψ Ω ΑΙ ΑΥ ΕΙ ΕΥ ΟΙ ΟΥ ΜΠ ΝΤ
β γ δ ζ η θ λ μ ν ξ π ρ σ υ φ χ ψ ω αι αυ ει ευ οι ου μπ ντ
v y th z i TH l m n x p r s i f H p s o e af i e f i oo b d

κ**αυτός** hot
κ**αφέ** brown
κ**αφενείο** (το) café
κ**αφές** (ο) coffee; καφές με
γάλα white coffee
κ**άψιμο** (το) burn
κ**έικ** (το) cake
Κ**ελσίου** centigrade
κ**έλυφος** (το) shell
κ**εντρική θέρμανση** (η)
central heating
κ**έντρο** (το) centre
κ**εράσι** (το) cherry
κ**ερδίζω** earn; win
κ**ερί** (το) candle
Κ**έρκυρα** (η) Corfu
κ**εφάλι** (το) head
κ**ηδεία** (η) funeral
κ**ήπος** (ο) garden
κ**ιβώτιο ταχυτήτων** (το)
gearbox
κ**ιθάρα** (η) guitar
κ**ιλό** (το) kilo
κ**ιμάς** (ο) minced meat
κ**ίνδυνος** (ο) danger
κ**ινηματογραφική μηχανή** (η)
cine camera
κ**ίτρινος** yellow
KKE Greek Communist
Party
κ**λαίω** cry
κ**λάξον** (το) horn (in car)
κ**λασσική μουσική** (η)
classical music
κ**λέβω** steal
κ**λειδαριά** (η) lock
κ**λειδί** (το) key; spanner
κ**λειδώνω** lock
κ**λείνω** close; switch off
κ**λείνω θέση** reserve
κ**λειστός** closed; off (lights)

κ**λέφτης** (ο) thief
κ**λίμα** (το) climate
κ**λιματιζόμενος** air-
conditioned
κ**λιματισμός** (ο) air-
conditioning
κ**λοπή** (η) theft
κ**λωστή** (η) thread
κ**όβω** cut
κ**οιλάδα** (η) valley
κ**οιμάμαι** sleep; be asleep
κ**οινωνία** (η) society
κ**οκκαλιάρης** skinny
κ**όκκαλο** (το) bone
κ**οκκινομάλης** (ο) red-head
κ**όκκινος** red
κ**οκκύτης** (ο) whooping cough
κ**οκτέηλ** (το) cocktail
κ**όλλα** (η) glue
κ**ολλιέ** (το) necklace
κ**όλπος** (ο) vagina; gulf
κ**ολυμπώ** swim
κ**ολύμπι** (το) swimming
κ**ολώνια** (η) eau de toilette
κ**ολώνια μετά το ξύρισμα** (η)
aftershave
κ**ομμάτι** (το) piece
κ**ομμώτρια** (η) hairdresser
κ**ομπιουτεράκι** (το)
calculator
κ**ομπολόι** (το) worry beads
κ**ονιάκ** (το) brandy
κ**οντά** near; εδώ κοντά
near here
κ**οντέρ** (το) speedometer
κ**οντινός** near
κ**οντίσιονερ** (το) conditioner
κ**οντός** short (person)
κ**ορδόνια παπουτσιών** (τα)
shoe laces
κ**όρη** (η) daughter

κορίτσι (το) girl
κόρνα (η) horn (in car)
κορυφή (η) top
κοσμήματα (τα) jewellery
κόσμος (ο) world; people, crowd
κόστος (το) cost; κοστίζει it costs
κοτόπουλο (το) chicken
κουβάς (ο) bucket
κουβέρτα (η) blanket
κουδούνι (το) bell (for door)
κουζίνα (η) cooker; kitchen
κουκέτα (η) couchette
κουκέτες (οι) bunk beds
κούκλα (η) doll
κουμπί (το) button
κουνέλι (το) rabbit
κούνια (η) cot
κουνούπι (το) mosquito
κουνουπίδι (το) cauliflower
κουπέ (το) compartment
κουρασμένος tired
κουρέας (ο) barber
κούρεμα (το) haircut
κουρτίνα (η) curtain
κουστούμι (το) suit
κουτάλι (το) spoon
κουτί (το) box; can
κουφός deaf
κραγιόν (το) lipstick
κράμπα (η) cramp
κρανίο (το) skull
κρασί (το) wine;
  κόκκινο/άσπρο/ροζέ κρασί red/white/rosé wine
κρασί του μαγαζιού (το) house wine
κρατώ hold; keep
κράτηση θέσης (η) reservation
κρέας (το) meat
κρεβάτι (το) bed; μονό/διπλό

κρεβάτι single/double bed
κρέμα (η) cream
κρέμα προσώπου (η) face cream
κρεμάστρα (η) coathanger
κρεμμύδι (το) onion
κρέπα (η) pancake
Κρήτη (η) Crete
κρίμα: είναι κρίμα it's a pity
κρουαζιέρα (η) cruise
κρύβομαι hide
κρύβω hide
κρύο (το) cold; κάνει κρύο it's cold
κρύος cold (adjective)
κρύωμα (το) cold;
  είμαι κρυωμένος I have a cold
κτηνίατρος (ο) vet
κτίριο (το) building
κυβέρνηση (η) government
κυβερνήτης (ο) captain
κυκλοφορία (η) traffic
κυκλοφοριακή συμφόρηση (η) traffic jam
κύμα (το) wave
κυνήγι (το) game (meat)
κυνηγώ hunt
Κύπρος (η) Cyprus
κυρία (η) lady; Madam
Κυρία (η) Mrs; Ms
Κυριακή (η) Sunday
κύριε sir
κύριος main
κύριος (ο) gentleman
Κύριος (ο) Mr
κύστη (η) bladder
κυττάζω look
κώδικας κυκλοφορίας (ο) highway code
κωδικός αριθμός (ο) dialling code

Β Γ Δ Ζ Η Θ   Λ Μ Ν Ξ   Π Ρ Σ Υ Φ Χ Ψ Ω   ΑΙ   ΑΥ ΕΙ   ΕΥ   ΟΙ   ΟΥ ΜΠ ΝΤ
β γ δ ζ η θ   λ μ ν ξ   π ρ σ υ φ χ ψ ω   αι   αυ ει   ευ   οι   ου μπ   ντ
v y th z i TH   l m n x   p r s i f H ps o e   af   i efi   oo   b   d

Λλ

λάδι (το) oil

λάδι μαυρίσματος (το) suntan oil

λαδόξυδο (το) salad dressing (oil and vinegar)

λάθος (το) mistake

λάθος wrong

λαιμός (ο) neck; throat

λακ (η) hair lacquer

λάμπα (η) light bulb; lamp

λαστιχάκι (το) rubber band

λάστιχο (το) rubber (material); tyre; σκασμένο λάστιχο flat tyre

λαχανικά (τα) vegetables

λάχανο (το) cabbage

λεβιές ταχυτήτων (ο) gear lever

λείπω be missing; not be in; be away; μου λείπεις I miss you

λειτουργία (η) mass (church)

λεκές (ο) stain

λεμονάδα (η) lemonade

λεμόνι (το) lemon

λέξη (η) word

λεξικό (το) dictionary

λεπτό (το) minute

λεπτός slim

λέσχη (η) club

λευκοπλάστ (το) Elastoplast (R)

λεφτά (τα) money

λέω say; λένε ότι they say that; πως σε λένε; what's your name?; με λένε . . . my name is . . .

λεωφορείο (το) bus

λιακάδα (η) sunshine

λίγα a few

λίγο a little bit; λίγοι τουρίστες few tourists

λίγος little; short

λιγότερο less

λικέρ (το) liqueur

λιμάνι (το) harbour

λίμα νυχιών (η) nailfile

λίμνη (η) lake

λιμνούλα (η) pond

λιπαρός greasy

λιποθυμώ faint

λίρα (η) pound (sterling)

λίμπρα (η) pound (weight)

λίτρο (το) litre

λογαριασμός (ο) bill

λογικός sensible

Λονδίνο (το) London

λόξυγγας (ο) hiccups

λουκάνικο (το) sausage

λουλούδι (το) flower

λουτρό (το) bathroom

λόφος (ο) hill

λυπάμαι I'm sorry

λυπημένος sad

Μμ

μαγαζί (το) shop

μαγειρεύω cook

μαγειρικά σκεύη (τα) cooking utensils

μάγειρος (ο), μαγείρισα (η) cook

μαγιό (το) swimming trunks/costume

μαγιονέζα (η) mayonnaise

104

GREEK-ENGLISH

μαζί together
μαθαίνω learn
μάθημα (το) lesson; κανω
  μάθημα teach; take a
  lesson
Μάιος (ο) May
μακαρόνια (τα) pasta
μακριά far (away)
μακρύς long
μαλακός soft
μάλιστα yes; μάλιστα!
  well!
μαλλί (το) wool
μαλλιά (τα) hair
μάλλον rather; probably
μαλώνω fight
μαμά (η) mum
μανάβης (ο) greengrocer
μανιτάρια (τα) mushrooms
μανό (το) nail polish
μανταλάκι (το) clothes peg
μαντήλι (το) handkerchief;
  headscarf
μαξιλάρι (το) pillow
μαργαρίνη (η) margarine
μαρκαδόρος (ο) felt-tip pen
μαρμελάδα (η) jam;
  marmalade
μαρούλι (το) lettuce
Μάρτιος (ο) March
μάρτυρας (ο) witness
μασέλα (η) dentures
μάσκαρα (η) mascara
μας us; our
μάτι (το) eye; ring (on
  cooker)
ματς (το) match (sport)
μαυρίζω tan
μαύρισμα (το) tan (colour)
μαύρος black
μαχαίρι (το) knife
μαχαιροπήρουνα (τα) cutlery
με with; by; me

μεγάλος big
μέγεθος (το) size
μεγένθυση (η) enlargement
μεθαύριο the day after
  tomorrow
μεθυσμένος drunk
μέικ απ (το) make-up
μελανιά (η) bruise
μέλι (το) honey
μέλισσα (η) bee
μελιτζάνα (η) aubergine
μέλλον (το) · future
μενού (το) menu
μένω live; stay
μέρα (η) day
μερίδα (η) portion
μερικοί, μερικές, μερικά
  some
μέρος (το) part
μέσα in; inside
μεσάνυχτα (τα) midnight
μέση (η) middle; waist
μεσημέρι (το) midday
Μεσόγειος (η)
  Mediterranean
μετά after; afterwards
μετακινούμαι move
μεταλλικό νερό (το) mineral
  water
μέταλλο (το) metal
μετάξι (το) silk
μεταξύ between
μεταφέρω carry
μεταφράζω translate
μετεωρολογικό δελτίο (το)
  weather forecast
μετρητά (τα) cash; τοις
  μετρητοίς in cash
μέτριος medium; average
μέτρο (το) metre
μέτωπο (το) forehead
μέχρι until
μηδέν zero

105

ΒΓΔΖΗΘ ΛΜΝΞΠΡΣΥΦΧΨΩ ΑΙ ΑΥ ΕΙ ΕΥ ΟΙ ΟΥ ΜΠ ΝΤ
β γ δ ζ η θ λ μ ν ξ π ρ σ υ φ χ ψ ω αι αν ει ευ οι ου μπ ντ
v y th z i TH l m n x p r s i f H͵ ps o e af i e f i oo b d

μη don't
μη καπνίζοντες non-smoking
μήκος (το) length
μήλο (το) apple
μηλόπιτα (η) apple pie
μήνας (ο) month
μήνας του μέλιτος (ο)
  honeymoon
μητέρα (η) mother
μητριά (η) stepmother
μητρόπολη (η) cathedral
μηχανάκι (το) moped
μηχανή (η) engine
μηχανικός (ο) mechanic;
  engineer
μια a; one
μίζα (η) ignition
μικρό όνομα (το) Christian
  name
μικρός little, small
μιλώ speak; μιλάτε..., do
  you speak...?
μισός half; μισή ώρα half
  an hour; μισό λίτρο/μισή
  μέρα half a litre/day
μισοψημένο medium (steak)
μισώ hate
μ.μ. (μετά μεσημβρίας) p.m.
μνημείο (το) monument
μόδα (η) fashion; της
  μόδας fashionable
μοιάζει it looks/seems;
μοιράζομαι share
μοκέτα (η) carpet (fitted)
μολύβι (το) pencil
μόλυνση (η) infection
μολυσμένος polluted
μόνο only
μονό δωμάτιο (το) single
  room
μονοπάτι (το) path

μόνος alone
μοντέρνος modern
μοσχάρι (το) beef; veal
μοτοσυκλέτα (η) motorbike
μου my
μουσείο (το) museum
μουσική (η) music
μουσική ποπ (η) pop music
μουσικό όργανο (το) musical
  instrument
μουστάκι (το) moustache
μουστάρδα (η) mustard
μπαίνω go in, enter
μπακάλικο (το) grocer's
μπαλκόνι (το) balcony
μπάλα (η) ball (large)
μπαλλάκι (το) ball (small)·
μπαμπάς (ο) dad
μπανάνα (η) banana
μπανιέρα (η) bathtub
μπάνιο (το) bath; bathe;
  πάω για μπάνιο go
  swimming
μπαρ (το) bar
μπάρμαν (ο) barman
μπαταρία (η) battery
μπαχαρικό (το) spice
μπεζ beige
μπέικον (το) bacon
μπέημπι-σίττερ (η) baby-sitter
μπερδεμένος complicated
μπιζέλια (τα) peas
μπικίνι (το) bikini
μπισκότο (το) biscuit
μπλε blue
μπλούζα (η) blouse
μπλουζάκι (το) T-shirt
μπόρα (η) shower (rain)
μπορώ I can; μπορείτε
  να/μπορείς να...; can you
  ...?

106

μπότα (η) boot (*shoe*)
μπουγάδα (η) washing;
  βάζω μπουγάδα do the
  washing
μπουζί (το) spark plug
μπουκάλι (το) bottle
μπουκιά (η) bite
μπούτι (το) thigh
μπριζόλα (η) chop (*meat*)
μπροστα από in front of
μπροστινό μέρος (το) front
μπύρα (η) beer, lager
μπωλ (το) bowl
μύγα (η) fly
μύδια (τα) mussels
μυθιστόρημα (το) novel
μυρίζω smell (*verb*)
μυρμήγκι (το) ant
μυρωδιά (η) smell
μυστικός secret
μυς (ο) muscle
μύτη (η) nose
μύωπας shortsighted
μωβ purple
μωρό (το) baby

Nν

να here is/are
ναι yes
νάυλον κάλτσες (οι)
  stockings
νάιτκλαμπ (το) nightclub
ναρκωτικά (τα) drugs
ΝΔ New Democracy
  (Conservative)
νέα (τα) news
νεκροταφείο (το) cemetery
Νέο Ετος (το) New Year
νέοι (οι) young people
νέος new; young

νέος (ο) teenager
νερό (το) water
νεροχύτης (ο) sink
νέσκαφε (το) instant coffee
νευρικός nervous
νευρικός κλονισμός (ο)
  nervous breakdown
νευρωτικός neurotic
νεφρά (τα) kidneys
νησί (το) island
νιπτήρας (ο) washbasin
νιώθω feel
Νοέμβριος (ο) November
νοικιάζω rent
νομίζω ότι . . . I think that . . .
νόμος (ο) law
νοσοκόμα (η) nurse
νοσοκομείο (το) hospital
νοσταλγώ I'm homesick
νόστιμος tasty
νοστιμότατος delicious
νότια (από) south (of)
νότος (ο) south
ντεπόζιτο (το) tank
ντήζελ (το) diesel
ντισκοτέκ (η) disco
ντιστριμπυτέρ (το)
  distributor
ντομάτα (η) tomato
ντουλάπι (το) cupboard
ντους (το) shower
ντρέπομαι I feel ashamed
ντροπαλός shy
ντύνομαι dress (*oneself*)
ντύνω dress (*someone*)
νυστάζω I'm sleepy
νύφη (η) daughter-in-law;
  sister-in-law; bride
νύχι (το) fingernail
νυχοκόπτης (ο) nail clippers
νύχτα (η) night
νυχτικό (το) nightdress
νωρίς early

B Γ Δ Z H Θ Λ M N Ξ Π P Σ Y Φ X Ψ Ω AI AY EI EY OI OY MΠ NT
β γ δ ζ η θ λ μ ν ξ π ρ σ υ φ χ ψ ω αι αυ ει ευ οι θυ μπ ντ
v y th z i TH l m n x p r s i f H ps o e af i efi oo b d

ξαδέλφη (η) cousin (*female*)
ξάδελφος (ο) cousin (*male*)
ξανά again
ξανθός blond
ξαπλώνω lie down
ξαφνικά suddenly
ξεκουράζομαι relax
ξεναγός (ο) guide
ξενοδοχείο (το) hotel
ξένος foreign
ξενώνας νέων (ο) youth
    hostel
ξέρω know; δεν ξέρω I
    don't know
ξεφωνίζω scream
ξεχνώ leave; forget
ξεχωριστά separately
ξηρός dry
ξοδεύω spend
ξύδι (το) vinegar
ξύλο (το) wood
ξινός sour
ξυπνώ wake up
ξυπνητήρι (το) alarm clock
ξύπνιος awake
ξυραφάκι (το) razor
ξυρίζομαι shave
ξυριστική μηχανή (η) electric
    shaver
ξύστρα (η) pencil sharpener

o the
OA Olympic Airways

ΟΑΣΘ Thessaloniki Public
    Transport Corporation
οδηγώ drive
οδηγός (ο) car driver
οδικά έργα (τα) roadworks
οδοντόβουρτσα (η) toothbrush
οδοντογιατρός (ο) dentist
οδοντόκρεμα (η) toothpaste
οδός (η) road, street
οδυνηρός painful
όζα (η) nail polish
οι the
οικογένεια (η) family
Οκτώβριος (ο) October
Ολλανδία (η) Holland
Ολλανδικός Dutch
όλος, όλη, όλο all; whole;
    όλα πληρωμένα all inclusive
όλοι everyone
ολόκληρος whole
ομάδα (η) group; team
ομάδα αίματος (η) blood group
ομελέτα (η) scrambled eggs;
    omelette
ομίχλη (η) fog
όμοιος similar; same
όμορφος fine
ομοφυλόφιλος gay
ομπρέλλα (η) umbrella
όνειρο (το) dream
όνομα (το) name; first name
όπερα (η) opera
όπισθεν (η) reverse (gear)
όπλο (το) gun; rifle
οποίος who; του οποίου
    whose
οπτικός (ο) optician
όπως like; as; όπως και
    νάναι anyway
οργανωμένη εκδρομή (η)
    package tour

GREEK-ENGLISH

οργανώνω organize
όρεξη (η) appetite; καλή όρεξη! enjoy your meal!
όριο ταχύτητας (το) speed limit
όροφος (o) floor, storey
ορχήστρα (η) orchestra
ΟΣΕ Greek Railways
οστρακοειδή (τα) shellfish
όταν when
ΟΤΕ Greek Telecommunications
οτιδήποτε anything; whatever
Ουαλλή (η) Welshwoman
Ουαλλία Wales
Ουαλλικός Welsh
Ουαλλός (o) Welshman
ΟΥΘ Thessaloniki Water Board
ουίσκυ (το) whisky
ουρά (η) queue; tail; κάνω ουρά queue
ουράνιο τόξο (το) rainbow
ουρανός (o) sky
ούτε... ούτε... neither... nor...
όχημα (το) vehicle
όχι no; not

Ππ

παγάκι (το) ice cube
πάγος (o) ice
παγωτό (το) ice cream
παγωτό ξυλάκι (o) ice lolly
παιδί (το) child
παίζω play
παίρνω get; take
παιχνίδι (το) game; toy
πακέτο (το) package; packet
παλαιοπωλείο (το) antique

shop
παλάτι (το) palace
παλιός old (thing)
παλίρροια (η) tide
παλτό (το) coat
Πάμπερς (τα) (R) nappy-liners
πάνα (η) nappy
πανεπιστήμιο (το) university
πανηγύρι (το) fair, funfair
πανί (το) sail
πανικός (o) panic
πανκ punk
πανσιόν (η) guesthouse
πάντα always; still
πανταλόνι (το) trousers
παντζούρια (τα) shutters
πάντοτε always
παντού everywhere
παντόφλες (οι) slippers
παντρεμμένος married
πάνω on; up; upstairs; πάνω από above
παξιμάδι (το) nut (for bolt)
παπάς (o) priest
Πάπας (o) Pope
πάπια (η) duck
πάπλωμα (το) quilt
παπούτσι (το) shoe
παππούς (o) grandfather
παραγγελία (η) message
παραγγέλνω order
παράδειγμα (το) example; παραδείγματος χάρι for example
παράδοση (η) tradition
παραδοσιακός traditional
παράθυρο (το) window
παρακαλώ please; excuse me; you're welcome
παραλία (η) beach
παραμάνα (η) safety pin
παραμένω stay, remain

109

ΒΓΔΖΗΘ Λ Μ Ν Ξ Π Ρ Σ Υ Φ Χ Ψ Ω ΑΙ ΑΥ ΕΙ ΕΥ ΟΙ ΟΥ ΜΠ ΝΤ
β γ δ ζ η θ λ μ ν ξ π ρ σ υ φ χ ψ ω αι αυ ει ευ οι ου μπ ντ
v y th z i TH l m n x p r s i f H p s o e af i e f i oo b d

παράξενος   strange
παραπέρα   further
πάρα πολύ   too much; very
 much
παραπονούμαι   complain
Παρασκευή (η)   Friday
παρατηρώ   watch
παρατσούκλι (το)   nickname
παρεξήγηση (η)
 misunderstanding
παρκάρω   park
πάρκινγκ (το)   car park
πάρκο (το)   park
παρμπρίζ (το)   windscreen
πάρτυ (το)   party, celebration
ΠΑΣΟΚ   Panhellenic
 Socialist Movement
πάστα (η)   tart
παστίλιες λαιμού (οι)   throat
 pastilles
Πάσχα (το)   Easter
πατάτα (η)   potato
πατέρας (ο)   father
πατερίτσες (οι)   crutches
πατριός (ο)   stepfather
πάτωμα (το)   floor (of room)
παυσίπονο (το)   painkiller
πάχος (το)   fat
παχύς   fat; thick
πάω   go; πάω στην/στο/στον
 ...   I'm going to ...; σου
 πάει το μπλε   blue suits you
πεζοδρόμιο (το)   pavement
πεζόδρομος (ο)   pedestrian
 precinct
πεζός (ο)   pedestrian
πεθαίνω   die
πεθαμένος   dead
πεθερά (η)   mother-in-law
πεθερός (ο)   father-in-law
πεινώ   I'm hungry

πειράζει   it matters; θα σε
 πείραζε αν ...   do you
 mind if I ...?; δεν πειράζει
 it doesn't matter
Πέμπτη (η)   Thursday
πενικιλλίνη (η)   penicillin
πέννα (η)   pen
πένσα (η)   pliers
πέος (το)   penis
πεπόνι (το)   melon
περάστε   come in!
περιμένω   wait
περιοδικό (το)   magazine
περίοδος (η)   period
περιοχή (η)   area
περίπατος (ο)   walk; πάω
 περίπατο   go for a walk
περίπου   about
περισσότερο   more
περισσότερο (το)   most (of)
περμανάντ (η)   perm
περνώ   cross, go through
περπατώ   walk
πέρσι   last year
πετάλι (το)   pedal
πεταλούδα (η)   butterfly
πετώ   throw away
πέτρα (η)   stone
πετσέτα (η)   napkin; towel
πετσέτα κουζίνας (η)   tea
 towel
πετώ   fly
πέφτω   fall
πηγή (η)   fountain
πηγούνι (το)   chin
πηδώ   jump
πηρούνι (το)   fork
πιάνω   catch; με πιάνει η
 θάλασσα   I get seasick
πιατάκι (το)   saucer
πιατικά (τα)   crockery

πιάτο (το)   dish; plate
πιθανώς   probably
πικάντικος   spicy
πικάπ (το)   record player
πικρός   bitter
πιλότος (ο)   pilot
πινακίδα (η)   road sign
πινακίδες (οι)   number plate
πινακοθήκη (η)   art gallery
πινγκπόνγκ (το)   table tennis
πινέλο (το)   paint brush
πινέλο γιά ξύρισμα (το)
   shaving brush
πίνω   drink
πιο   more
πίπα (η)   pipe (to smoke)
πιπέρι (το)   pepper (spice)
πιπεριά (η)   pepper (vegetable)
πισίνα (η)   swimming pool
πιστεύω   believe
πιστολάκι (το)   hair dryer
πιστόλι (το)   gun, pistol
πιστοποιητικό (το)   certificate
πιστωτική κάρτα (η)   credit
   card
πίσω   back; behind
πίσω φώτα (τα)   rear lights
πίτσα (η)   pizza
πίττα (η)   pie; sloshed
πλαστική σακούλα (η)   plastic
   bag
πλαστικός   plastic
πλατεία (η)   square (in town)
πλάτη (η)   back (of body)
πλατύς   wide
πλατφόρμα (η)   platform
πλέκω   knit
πλένομαι   wash
πλένω   wash
πλευρά (η)   side
πλευρό (το)   rib
πληγή (η)   wound
πλήθος (το)   crowd

πληροφορίες (οι)   directory
   enquiries; information
πλήρωμα (το)   crew
πληρώνω   pay
πλοίο (το)   boat, ship
πλούσιος   rich
πλυντήριο (το)   washing
   machine
πλυντήριο ρούχων (το)
   launderette
πλύσιμο των πιάτων (το)
   washing-up
πνεύμονες (οι)   lungs
πνευμονία (η)   pneumonia
ποδηλασία (η)   cycling
ποδηλάτης (ο)   cyclist
ποδήλατο (το)   bicycle
πόδι (το)   foot; leg; με τα
   πόδια   on foot
ποδόσφαιρο (το)   football
ποιανού;   whose?
ποιό;   which?
ποιός;   who?
ποιότητα (η)   quality
πόλεμος (ο)   war
πόλη (η)   city, town
πολιτεία (η)   state
πολιτικά (τα)   politics
πολιτικός   political
πολλοί,   πολλές,   πολλά
   a lot (of)
πολύ   much; very; too
   much; too
πονάει   it hurts
πονόδοντος (ο)   toothache
πονοκέφαλος (ο)   headache
πόνος (ο)   ache, pain
ποντίκι (το)   mouse
πόνυ (το)   pony
πορεία (η)   route
πόρτα (η)   door
πορτ-μπαγκάζ (το)   boot (car)
πορτ-μπε-μπέ (το)   carry-cot

Β Γ Δ Ζ Η Θ Λ Μ Ν Ξ Π Ρ Σ Υ Φ Χ Ψ Ω ΑΙ ΑΥ ΕΙ ΕΥ ΟΙ ΟΥ ΜΠ ΝΤ
β γ δ ζ η θ λ μ ν ξ π ρ σ υ φ χ ψ ω αι αυ ει ευ οι ου μπ ντ
v y th z i TH l m n x p r s i f H p s o e af i e f i oo b d

πορτοκάλι (το) orange
πορτοκαλί orange
πορτοφολάς (ο) pickpocket
πορτοφόλι (το) wallet
πόσιμο νερό (το) drinking water
πόσοι, πόσες, πόσα; how many?
πόσος, πόση, πόσο; how much?; πόσο κάνει; how much does it cost?
πόστερ (το) poster
ποστ ρεστάντ poste restante
ποτάμι (το) river
ποτέ never
πότε; when?
ποτήρι (το) glass
ποτό (το) drink
που that; who
πού; where?
πούδρα ταλκ (η) talc
πουθενά nowhere
πουκάμισο (το) shirt
πουλερικά (τα) poultry
πουλί (το) bird
πούλμαν (το) coach
πουλόβερ (το) jumper
πουλώ sell
πούρο (το) cigar
πράγμα (το) thing
πραγματικά really
πρακτικός practical
πρακτορείο (το) agency
πρακτορείο λεωφορείων (το) bus station
πράσινος green
πρέπει να . . . I have to . . .
πρεσβεία (η) embassy
πρησμένος swollen
πρίγκηπας (ο) prince
πριγκίπισσα (η) princess

πρίζα (η) socket;. plug
πρίζα ταυ (η) adaptor
πριν before; πριν τρεις μέρες three days ago
προάστια (τα) suburbs
πρόβατο (το) sheep
πρόβλημα (το) problem
προβλήτα (η) quay
προβολείς (οι) headlights
πρόγονος (ο) ancestor
πρόγραμμα (το) programme; timetable
προκαταβολή (η) advance
προκαταβολικά in advance
προξενείο (το) consulate
προσβάλλω offend
προσεχτικός careful
πρόσεξε! look out!
προσέχω take care of
προσκαλώ invite
πρόσκληση (η) invitation
προσπέκτους (το) brochure
προσπερνώ overtake
προστατεύω protect
πρόστιμο (το) fine
προσφέρω offer
πρόσωπο (το) face
προτείνω recommend
προτεραιότητα (η) right of way
προτιμώ prefer
προφανής obvious
προφέρω pronounce
προφορά (η) accent
προφυλακτήρας (ο) bumper
προφυλακτικό (το) condom
προχτές the day before yesterday
πρωί (το) morning
πρωινό (το) breakfast
πρώτα first, firstly

πρώτες βοήθειες (οι) first aid
πρώτη θέση first class
πρώτο πάτωμα (το) first floor
πρώτος first
πρώτο πιάτο (το) starter
Πρωτοχρονιά (η) New
  Year's Day
πτήση (η) flight
πτήση τσάρτερ (η) charter
  flight
πυξίδα (η) compass
πύργος (ο) tower
πυρετός (ο) fever
πυρκαγιά (η) fire
πυροσβεστήρας (ο) fire
  extinguisher
πυροσβεστική υπηρεσία (η)
  fire brigade
πυροτεχνήματα (τα) fireworks
πυτζάμες (οι) pyjamas
πωλείται for sale
πώληση (η) sale
πώς; how?; πώς πάει; how
  are things?

ράβω sew
ραδιόφωνο (το) radio
ραντεβού (το) appointment
ράντζο (το) campbed
ρεζέρβα (η) spare tyre
ρεσεψιόν (η) reception
ρεσεψιονίστ (η/ο)
  receptionist
ρεύμα (το) current; draught
ρευματισμοί (οι) rheumatism
ρίχνω throw
ρόδα (η) wheel
ροδάκινο (το) peach

Ρόδος (η) Rhodes
ροζ pink
ροκ (η) rock music
ρολόι (το) clock; watch
ρόμπα (η) dressing gown
ρούμι (το) rum
ρούχα (τα) clothes
ροχαλίζω snore
ρύζι (το) rice
ρυμούλκα (η) trailer (for car)
ρωτώ ask

Σάββατο (το) Saturday
Σαββατοκύριακο (το)
  weekend
σαγόνι (το) jaw
σακάκι (το) jacket
σακβουαγιάζ (το) hand
  luggage
σακίδιο (το) rucksack
σάκος (ο) backpack
σαλάτα (η) salad
σαλιγκάρι (το) snail
σαλόνι (το) lounge
σάλτσα (η) sauce
σαμπουάν (το) shampoo
σαμπρέλα (η) inner tube
σαν like, as
σανδάλια (τα) sandals
σαντιγί (η) whipped cream
σάντουιτς (το) sandwich
σάουνα (η) sauna
σάπιος rotten
σαπούνι (το) soap
σαπούνι πιάτων (το)
  washing-up liquid
σαρδέλλα (η) sardine
σας you; your
σβήνω switch off (engine);

Β Γ Δ Ζ Η Θ Λ Μ Ν Ξ Π Ρ Σ Υ Φ Χ Ψ Ω ΑΙ ΑΥ ΕΙ ΕΥ ΟΙ ΟΥ ΜΠ ΝΤ
β γ δ ζ η θ λ μ ν ξ π ρ σ υ φ χ ψ ω αι αυ ει ευ οι ου μπ ντ
v y th z i TH l m n x p r s i f H p s o e af i e f i oo b d

put out *(fire)*
οβήστρα (η) rubber, eraser
σεζ λονγχ (η) deckchair
σελίδα (η) page
σέλλοτεηπ (το) sellotape *(R)*
σελφ σέρβις self-service
σεντόνι (το) sheet
σεξ (το) sex
σέξυ sexy
Σεπτέμβριος (ο) September
σερβιέτα (η) sanitary towel
σερβιτόρα (η) barmaid;
    waitress
σερβιτόρος (ο) waiter
σημαδούρα (η) buoy
σημαία (η) flag
σημειωματάριο (το)
    notebook
σήμερα today
σήραγγα (η) tunnel
σιγά-σιγά slowly
σίγουρος sure
σίδερο (το) iron
σιδερώνω iron
σιδηρόδρομος (ο) railway
σικότι (το) liver
σινεμά (το) cinema
σιωπή (η) silence
σκάλα (η) ladder
σκάλες (οι) stairs
σκέπτομαι think
σκηνή (η) tent
σκι ski
σκιά (η) shade, shadow
σκιά ματιών (η) eye shadow
σκληρός hard
σκόνη πλυντηρίου (η)
    washing powder
σκόρδο (το) garlic
σκοτεινός dark
σκοτώνω kill

σκουλαρίκια (τα) earrings
σκούπα (η) broom
σκουπίδια (τα) rubbish
σκουπιδοντενεκές (ο) dustbin
σκύλος (ο) dog
σκωληκοειδίτις (η)
    appendicitis
Σκωτία (η) Scotland
Σκωτσέζικος Scottish
σλάιντ (το) slide
σλήπιν-μπαγκ (το) sleeping
    bag
σλίπ (το) panties;
    underpants
σοβαρός serious
σοκ (το) shock
σοκολάτα (η) chocolate;
    σοκολάτα γάλακτος milk
    chocolate
σόλα (η) sole *(of shoe)*
σολομός (ο) salmon
σόμπα (η) oil heater
σορτς (το) shorts
σου you; your
σουγιάς (ο) penknife
σούπα (η) soup
σούπερμαρκετ (το)
    supermarket
σουτιέν (το) bra
σπάγγος (ο) string
σπανάκι (το) spinach
σπάνιος rare
σπασμένος broken
σπάω break
σπεσιαλιτέ (η) speciality
σπηλιά (η) cave
σπιράλ (το) spiral; IUD
σπίρτο (το) match *(light)*
σπίτι (το) house; στο σπίτι
    at home; για το σπίτι to
    take away *(food)*

114

σπορ (το) sport
σπουδαίος important
σπρώχνω push
σταγόνα (η) drop
σταθμός (ο) station
σταματώ stop; σταμάτα! stop!
στάση (η) stop
στάση λεωφορείου (η) bus stop
σταφύλια (τα) grapes
στέγη (η) roof
στεγνοκαθαριστήριο (το) dry-cleaner
στεγνός dry
στεγνώνω dry
στέλνω send
στενός narrow; tight
στενοχώρια (η) worry
στηθάγχη (η) angina
στήθος (το) breast; chest
στόμα (το) mouth
στομάχι (το) stomach
στον, στην, στο at; in; to; στον σταθμό at the station; στο Λονδίνο in London
στοπ! stop!
στρείδι (το) oyster
στριφτό (το) hand-rolled cigarette
στρογγυλός round
στρόφαλος (ο) crankshaft
στροφή (η) bend
στρώμα (το) mattress
στυλό (το) biro (R)
συγγενείς (οι) relatives
συγγνώμη excuse me; pardon?
σύγκρουση (η) crash
συγχαρητήρια! congratulations!
συγχωρώ: με συγχωρείτε excuse me

σύζυγος (ο) husband
συλλαμβάνω arrest
συλλογή (η) collection
συμβαίνω happen
συμβουλεύω advise
συμπεριλαμβάνεται included
συμπλέκτης (ο) clutch
συμφωνώ agree
συναγερμός (ο) alarm
συναγωγή (η) synagogue
συναίσθημα (το) feeling
συναλλαγματική ισοτιμία (η) exchange rate
συναντώ meet
συνάντηση (η) meeting
συναρπαστικός exciting
συναυλία (η) concert
σύνδεση (η) connection
συνήθεια (η) habit
συνηθισμένος usual
συνήθως usually
συννεφιασμένος cloudy
σύννεφο (το) cloud
συνοδεύω accompany
συνοικία (η) district
συνολικά altogether
σύνορα (τα) border
συνταγή (η) prescription; recipe
συνταξιούχος (ο) old-age pensioner
συντηρητικό διάλυμα (το) soaking solution
σύντομα soon
σύντομος δρόμος (ο) shortcut
σύρμα (το) wire
συστήνω introduce; recommend
συχνά often
σφήγγα (η) wasp
σφράγισμα (το) filling

Β Γ Δ Ζ Η Θ Λ Μ Ν Ξ Π Ρ Σ Υ Φ Χ Ψ Ω ΑΙ ΑΥ ΕΙ ΕΥ ΟΙ ΟΥ ΜΠ ΝΤ
β γ δ ζ η θ λ μ ν ξ π ρ σ υ φ χ ψ ω αι αυ ει ευ οι ου μπ ντ
v y th z i TH l m n x p r s i f H ps o e af i ef i oo b d

σφυρί *(το)* hammer
σχέδιο *(το)* plan
σχεδόν almost
σχοινί *(το)* rope
σχολείο *(το)* school
σωλήνας *(ο)* pipe *(water)*
σώμα *(το)* body
σωστός correct

Ττ

τα the; them
ταβάνι *(το)* ceiling
τα ινία *(η)* tape
τακούνι *(το)* heel *(of shoe)*
ταμείο *(το)* box office; cash
  desk
ταμπλέτα *(η)* tablet
ταμπόν *(το)* tampon
τάξη *(η)* class
ταξί *(το)* taxi
ταξιδεύω travel
ταξίδι *(το)* journey, trip; καλό
  ταξίδι have a good journey
ταξιδιωτική επιταγή *(η)*
  traveller's cheque
ταξιδιωτικό γραφείο *(το)*
  travel agent's
τάπα *(η)* plug *(in sink)*
τασάκι *(το)* ashtray
ταύρος *(ο)* bull
ταυτότητα *(η)* ID card
ταχυδρομείο *(το)* post office
ταχυδρόμος *(ο)* postman
ταχυδρομώ post
ταχύτητα *(η)* gear; speed
τέλειος perfect
τελειώνω finish
τελευταίος last

τελεφερίκ *(το)* cable car
τέλος *(το)* end
τελωνείο *(το)* customs
τεμπέλης lazy
τέννις *(το)* tennis
τέντα *(η)* tent, marquee
Τετάρτη *(η)* Wednesday
τέταρτο *(το)* quarter
τέχνη *(η)* art
τεχνητός artificial
τζαζ *(η)* jazz
τζηνς *(τα)* jeans
τζιν *(το)* gin; τζιν με τόνικ
  gin and tonic
τζόγγιγκ *(το)* jogging
ήγάνι *(το)* frying pan
τηγανίζω fry
τηγανιτές πατάτες *(οι)* chips
τηγανιτός fried
τηλεγράφημα *(το)* telegram
τηλεόραση *(η)* television
τηλεφώνημα κολλέκτ *(το)*
  reverse charge call
τηλεφωνικός θάλαμος *(ο)*
  phone box
τηλεφωνικός κατάλογος *(ο)*
  phone book
τηλέφωνο *(το)* telephone;
  παί ρνω τηλέφωνο phone
τηλεφωνώ ring, phone
την her
της her; hers; to her; of the
τι; what?; τι κάνεις; τι
  κάνετε; how are you?
τιμή *(η)* price
τίμιος honest
τιμόνι *(το)* steering wheel
τίποτε nothing
τις them; the
το in; it; the
τοίχος *(ο)* wall

τολμώ dare
τον him
τόννος (ο) tuna fish
τοπίο (το) landscape
τόσο so (much), that much;
  τόσο όμορφος όσο as
  beautiful as
τοστ (το) toasted sandwich
τότε then
του his; its; to him
τουαλέτα (η) toilet
τουαλέτα των γυναικών (η)
  ladies toilet
τούβλο (το) brick
τουλάχιστον at least
τουρίστας (ο) tourist
τουριστικός οδηγός (ο)
  guidebook
Τουρκία (η) Turkey
τους them; to them
τραβώ pull
τραγούδι (το) song
τραγουδώ sing
τράπεζα (η) bank
τραπεζαρία (η) dining room
τραπέζι (το) table
τραπεζομάντηλο (το)
  tablecloth
τραυματίζομαι hurt
τραυματισμένος injured
τρελλός mad
τρένο (το) train
τρέχω run
τριαντάφυλλο (το) rose
Τριτη (η) Tuesday
τρόλλεϋ (το) trolley
τρομερός tremendous
τροφική δηλητηρίαση (η)
  food poisoning
τροχονόμος (ο) traffic
  warden
τροχόσπιτο (το) caravan
τρύπα (η) hole

τρώω eat
τσαγιέρα (η) teapot
τσαγκάρης (ο) shoe repairer
τσάι (το) tea
τσάντα (η) bag; handbag
τσεκούρι (το) axe
τσέπη (η) pocket
τσιγάρο (το) cigarette
τσίμπημα (το) bite (insect)
τσιμπιδάκι (το) tweezers
τσιμπώ sting
τσιπς (τα) crisps
τσίχλα (η) chewing gum
τσόκ (το) choke (on car)
τσούχτρα (η) jellyfish
τυλίγω wrap
τυρί (το) cheese
τυφλός blind
τύχη (η) luck; καλή τύχη!
  good luck!; κατα τύχη by
  chance
τώρα now

υαλοκαθαριστήρας (ο)
  windscreen wiper
υγεία: στην υγειά σας/σου!
  your health!, cheers!
υγιής healthy
υγραέριο (το) Calor gas (R)
υγρός damp, wet
υδραυλικός (ο) plumber
υπάρχει/υπάρχουν there
  is/are
υπερβάλλω exaggerate
υπέρβαρο (το) excess
  baggage
υπερβολικά μεγάλο too big
υπερήφανος proud

117

Β Γ Δ Ζ Η Θ Λ Μ Ν Ξ Π Ρ Σ Υ Φ Χ Ψ Ω ΑΙ ΑΥ ΕΙ ΕΥ ΟΙ ΟΥ ΜΠ ΝΤ
β γ δ ζ η θ λ μ ν ξ π ϱ σ υ φ χ ψ ω αι αυ ει ευ οι ου μπ ντ
v y th z TH l m n x p r s i f H p s o e af i e f i oo b d

υπεύθυνος responsible
υπηρεσία (η) service
υπνοδωμάτιο (το) bedroom
ύπνος (ο) sleep
υπνωτικό χάπι (το) sleeping
  pill
υπόγειο (το) basement
υπόγειος (ο) underground
υπογράφω sign
υπολογιστής (ο) computer
υπόλοιπο (το) rest
υπόσχομαι promise
ύφασμα (το) material

Φφ

φαγητό (το) food; meal
φαγούρα (η) itch
φάκελος (ο) envelope
φακοί επαφής (οι) contact
  lenses
φακός (ο) lens; torch
φαλακρός bald
φαλλοκράτης (ο) male
  chauvinist
φανάρια τροχαίας (τα)
  traffic lights
φανταστικός fantastic
φαρμακείο (το) chemist's
φάρμακο (το) medicine
φάρος (ο) lighthouse
φασαρία (η) noise
φασολάκια (τα) green beans
φασόλια (τα) beans
Φεβρουάριος (ο) February
φεγγάρι (το) moon
φεμινίστρια (η) feminist
φερμουάρ (το) zip
φέρνω bring

φέρουμπωτ (το) ferry
φέτα (η) slice
φεύγω go away
φθινόπωρο (το) autumn
φίδι (το) snake
φιλώ kiss
φιλενάδα (η) girlfriend
φιλέτο (το) fillet steak
φιλί (το) kiss
φιλοδώρημα (το) service
  charge; tip
φιλοξενία (η) hospitality
φιλοξενούμενος (ο) guest
φίλος (ο) boyfriend; friend
φιλοφρόνηση (η)
  compliment
φίλτρο (το) filter
φιλμ (το) film
φλας (το) flash
φλερτάρω flirt
φλυτζάνι (το) cup
φοβάμαι be afraid
φοβερός terrible
φόβος (ο) fear
φοιτητής (ο) student (male)
φοιτήτρια (η) student
  (female)
φορά (η) time, occasion; μια
  φορά once
φόρεμα (το) dress
φορτηγό (το) lorry
φουντούκι (το) hazelnut
φούρνος (ο) oven
φουσκάλα (η) blister
φούστα (η) skirt
φρακαρισμένος blocked;
  stuck
φράκτης (ο) fence
φράουλα (η) strawberry
φρενάρω brake
φρένο (το) brake

GREEK-ENGLISH

φρέσκος fresh
φρικτός horrible
φρούτα (τα) fruit
φρυγανιά (η) toast
φρύδι (το) eyebrow
φταίω: εγώ φταίω/αυτός
  φταίει it's my/his fault
φτάνει that's enough
φτάνω arrive
φτέρνα (η) heel (of foot)
φτερνίζομαι sneeze
φτερό (το) wing
φτηνός cheap
φτυάρι (το) spade
φτωχός poor
φύγε! go away!
φύκια (τα) seaweed
φυλακή (η) prison
φύλλο (το) leaf
φύλο (το) gender
φύση (η) nature
φυσικός natural
φυσιολογικός normal
φυτό (το) plant
φωνάζω call; shout
φωνή (η) voice
φως (το) light
φώτα (τα) lights (on car)
φωτιά (η) fire; έχεις
  φωτιά; have you got a
  light?
φωτογραφία (η)
  photograph; βγάζω
  φωτογραφία photograph
φωτογραφική μηχανή (η)
  camera
φωτογράφος (ο)
  photographer
φωτόμετρο (το) light meter

χαλάκι (το) rug
χαλί (το) carpet
χαμηλά φώτα (τα) sidelights
χαμηλός low
χαμόγελο (το) smile
χαμογελώ smile
χάμπουργκερ (το)
  hamburger
χάνω lose; miss
χάπι (το) pill
χάρηκα pleased to meet you!
χάρπιχ (το) (R) bleach
χάρτης (ο) map
χαρτί (το) paper
χαρτιά (τα) playing cards
χαρτί υγείας (το) toilet paper
χαρτομάντηλα (τα) tissues
χαρτόνι (το) cardboard
χαρτονόμισμα (το) note
χαρτοπωλείο (το) stationer's
χαρτοφύλακας (ο) briefcase
χασάπης (ο) butcher's
χείλι (το) lip
χειμώνας (ο) winter
χειρότερος worse; ο
  χειρότερος worst
χειροτεχνία (η) crafts
χειρόφρενο (το) handbrake
χέρι (το) arm; hand
χερούλι (το) handle
χήνα (η) goose
χήρα (η) widow
χήρος (ο) widower
χθες yesterday
χιλιόμετρο (το) kilometre
χιόνι (το) snow
χιούμορ (το) humour
χλιαρός lukewarm
χλωρίνη (η) bleach

119

Β Γ Δ Ζ Η Θ Λ Μ Ν Ξ Π Ρ Σ Υ Φ Χ Ψ Ω ΑΙ ΑΥ ΕΙ ΕΥ ΟΙ ΟΥ ΜΠ ΝΤ
β γ δ ζ η θ λ μ ν ξ π ρ σ υ φ χ ψ ω αι αυ ει ευ οι ου μπ ντ
v y th z i TH l m n x p r s i f H ps o e af i ef i oo b d

χοιρινό (το) pork
χόμπυ (το) hobby
χορεύω dance
χορός (ο) dance
χορτάρι (το) grass
χορτοφάγος (ο) vegetarian
χρειάζομαι need
χρησιμοποιώ use
χρήσιμος useful
Χριστούγεννα (τα)
    Christmas; Καλά
    Χριστούγεννα! happy
    Christmas!
χρονιά (η) year; χρόνια
    πολλά happy birthday!
χρόνος (ο) time; year; του
    χρόνου next year; πόσο
    χρονών είσαι; how old are
    you?; είμαι 25 χρονών I'm
    25 years old
χρυσός (ο) gold
χρυσοχοείο (το) jeweller's
χρώμα (το) colour
χταπόδι (το) octopus
χτένα (η) comb
χτυπώ hit
χυμός (ο) juice
χώμα (το) earth
χωνί (το) funnel (for pouring)
χώρα (η) country
χωράφι (το) field
χωριό (το) village
χωρισμένος divorced
χωριστός separate
χωρίς without; χωρίς
    καφεΐνη decaffeinated
χώρος φύλαξης αποσκευών
    (ο) left luggage

ψαλίδι (το) scissors
ψαράδικο (το) fishmonger's
ψάρεμα (το) fishing
ψάρι (το) fish
ψάχνω look for
ψέματα: λέω ψέματα tell a lie
ψεύτικος false
ψηλός high; tall
ψήνω bake
ψητός στη σχάρα grilled
ψιλά (τα) small change
ψυγείο (το) fridge;
    ψυγείο αυτοκινήτου
    radiator (car)
ψύλλος (ο) ' flea
ψωμάκι (το) roll
ψωμί (ο) baker's
ψωμί (το) bread
ψώνια (τα) shopping; πάω
    για ψώνια go shopping

Ωω

ωμός raw
ώμος (ο) shoulder
ώρα (η) hour; τι ώρα
    είναι; what time is it?;
    στην ώρα του on time;
    στις τρεις η ώρα at three
    o'clock; σε λίγη ώρα soon
ωραίος beautiful;
    handsome; lovely
ώριμος ripe
ως as, since
ωτοστόπ (το) hitchhiking

GRAMMAR

There are three *GENDERS* in Greek — masculine, feminine and neuter. The *INDEFINITE ARTICLE* (a, an) for each gender is:

masc	fem	neut
ένας	μια	ένα
a temple	**a beer**	**a car**
ένας ναός	μια μπύρα	ένα αυτοκίνητο

The *DEFINITE ARTICLE* (the) is:

	masc	fem	neut
sing	ο	η	το
plural	οι	οι	τα

the grocer
η λεωφόρος

the avenue
ο μπακάλης

the grocery store
το μπακάλικο

the cars
τα αυτοκίνητα

There are three main *CASES* — nominative, genitive and accusative. The form of articles, nouns, adjectives and most pronouns varies according to their gender, number and case. The indefinite article (a, an) declines as follows:

sing	masc	fem	neut
nom	ένας	μια	ένα
gen	ενός	μιας	ενός
acc	ένα	μια	ένα

The definite article (the) declines as follows:

sing	masc	fem	neut
nom	ο	η	το
gen	του	της	του
acc	το(ν)	τη(ν)	το

plural			
nom	οι	οι	τα
gen	των	των	των
acc	τους	τις	τα

The *NOMINATIVE* is used for the subject of sentences:

the boss isn't here
το αφεντικό δεν είναι εδώ

GRAMMAR

The *GENITIVE* is used to indicate possession:

> **the boss's name**
> το όνομα του αφεντικού

The *ACCUSATIVE* is used for direct objects:

> **can I see the boss?**
> μπορώ να δω το αφεντικό;

The accusative is also used with certain prepositions (to, from, with etc):

> **where are you going?** – **to Athens**
> πού θα πάτε; – στην Αθήνα

> **where are you from?** – **from Britain**
> από πού είσαι; – από την Βρεταννία

> **we'll go by bus**
> θα πάμε με το λεωφορείο

There is also a *VOCATIVE* case which is used to address someone directly. This has the same endings as the nominative, apart from masculine nouns where the final ς is dropped:

> **where is Kostas?**   **Kostas, come here!**
> που είναι ο Κώστας;   Κώστα, έλα εδώ!

The endings of *NOUNS* change according to case and depending on whether they are used in the singular or *PLURAL*. In the following table regular **masculine** endings are shown for the three nouns ο άντρας (the man), ο ναύτης (the sailor) and ο ταχυδρόμος (the postman):

	-ας	-ης	-ος
sing			
nom	ο άντρας	ο ναύτης	ο ταχυδρόμος
gen	του άντρα	του ναύτη	του ταχυδρόμου
acc	τον άντρα	τον ναύτη	τον ταχυδρόμο
plural			
nom	οι άντρες	οι ναύτες	οι ταχυδρόμοι
gen	των αντρών	των ναυτών	των ταχυδρόμων
acc	τους άντρες	τους ναύτες	τους ταχυδρόμους

A few masculine nouns end in -ες or -ους, but for these only the plural differs from the above endings:

> ο καφές (coffee), *pl*: οι καφέδες
> ο παππούς (grandfather), *pl*: οι παππούδες

122

GRAMMAR

Feminine endings for nouns in either -α (η θάλασσα the sea) or
-η (η τέχνη art) are:

sing

nom	η θάλασσα	η τέχνη
gen	της θάλασσας	της τέχνης
acc	την θάλασσα	την τέχνη

plural nom	οι θάλασσες	οι τέχνες
gen	των θαλασσών	των τεχνών
acc	τις θάλασσες	τις τέχνες

But some feminine nouns ending in -η take a plural in -εις, for
example:

η πόλη	οι πόλεις
the city	**the cities**

Feminine nouns ending in -ος behave like masculine nouns.

Neuter endings for nouns in either -ο (το βιβλίο the book) or -ι
(το παιδί the child) or -μα (το γράμμα the letter) are:

singular

nom	το βιβλίο	το παιδί	το γράμμα
gen	του βιβλίου	του παιδιού	του γράμματος
acc	το βιβλίο	το παιδί	το γράμμα

plural

nom	τα βιβλία	τα παιδιά	τα γράμματα
gen	των βιβλίων	των παιδιών	των γραμμάτων
acc	τα βιβλία	τα παιδιά	τα γράμματα

Quite a few neuter nouns end in -ος (το δάσος the forest, *pl:* τα
δάση).

Most *ADJECTIVES* are formed with the following endings:

masc	*fem*	*neut*
καλός (good)	καλή	καλό

masc	*fem*	*neut*
πλούσιος (rich)	πλούσια	πλούσιο

Adjective endings follow the pattern of the corresponding
noun endings:

a nice coffee
ένας καλός καφές

we had a nice coffee
ήπιαμε ένα καλό καφέ

GRAMMAR

The *COMPARATIVE* is formed by putting the word πιο (more) in front of the adjective:

she is richer than Onassis
είναι πιο πλούσια από τον Ωνάση

The *SUPERLATIVE* is formed by putting the appropriate definite article in front of the comparative:

she is the richest woman in the world
είναι η πιο πλούσια γυναίκα του κόσμου

POSSESSIVE ADJECTIVES are:

my μου	our μας
your (*sing familiar*) σου	your (*plural/formal*) σας
his του	their τους
her της	
its του	

These are placed after the noun they refer to, with the definite article being placed in front:

my suitcases   **my wife**
οι βαλίτσες μου   η γυναίκα μου

her husband
ο άντρας της

PERSONAL PRONOUNS (I, you etc) decline as follows:

nom	gen	acc
εγώ I	μου me	με/εμένα me
εσύ you*	σου you	σε/εσένα you
αυτός he	του him	τον him
αυτή she	της her	την her
αυτό it	του it	το it
εμείς we	μας us	μας/εμάς us
εσείς you**	σας/εσάς you	σας/εσάς you
αυτοί they (*m*)	τους them	τους/αυτούς them
αυτές they (*f*)	τους them	τις/αυτές them
αυτά they (*n*)	τους them	τα/αυτά them

I brought her home
την έφερα στο σπίτι

who is it? — me
ποιός είναι; — εγώ

* This is the singular familiar form for *YOU*; use it only with people you are friendly with; ** this is the polite form (both singular and plural).

124

GRAMMAR

Where two forms are given for the accusative, the second is
used after prepositions:

that's for me
αυτό είναι για εμένα

he left without me
έφυγε χωρίς εμένα

In Greek personal pronouns are usually omitted as subjects:

I'm staying in Lindos
μένω στην Λίνδο

she's my sister
είναι η αδελφή μου

But they are used for emphasis:

HE did it!
αυτός το έκανε!

POSSESSIVE PRONOUNS (mine, hers etc) are formed by
placing the word δικός in front of the possessive adjective.
δικός declines like an adjective, agreeing with the object
possessed:

	masc	fem	neut
mine	δικός μου	δική μου	δικό μου
yours	δικός σου	δική σου	δικό σου
(fam)			
his	δικός του	δική του	δικό του
hers	δικός της	δική της	δικό της
its	δικός του	δική του	δικό του
ours	δικός μας	δική μας	δικό μας
yours	δικός σας	δική σας	δικό σας
(plural/polite)			
theirs	δικός τους	δική τους	δικό τους

Plurals take the usual adjective endings:

those towels are ours
αυτά τα προσόψια είναι δικά μας

our children are younger than yours
τα παιδιά μας είναι πιο μικρά απο τα δικά σας

In dictionaries *VERBS* are listed in the first person singular of
the present tense. This is the basic form (equivalent to the
infinitive in English) and the endings are either -ω or -μαι.

GRAMMAR

PRESENT TENSE endings for verbs ending in -ω are of two types depending on whether or not the stress falls on the last syllable:

	stress not on last syllable πληρώνω (I pay)	stress on last syllable μιλώ (I speak)
I	πληρώνω	μιλώ
you	πληρώνεις	μιλάς
he/she	πληρώνει	μιλά
we	πληρώνουμε	μιλάμε
you	πληρώνετε	μιλάτε
they	πληρώνουν	μιλούν

how much are you paying?
πόσο πληρώνεις;

Present tense endings for verbs ending in -μαι are:

	πληρώνομαι (I am paid)
I	πληρώνομαι
you	πληρώνεσαι
he/she	πληρώνεται
we	πληρωνόμαστε
you	πληρωνόσαστε
they	πληρώνονται

Two common and useful verbs are irregular:

είμαι (I am)

είμαι I am	είμαστε we are
είσαι you are	είσαστε you are
είναι he/she/it is	είναι they are

έχω (I have)

έχω I have	έχουμε we have
έχεις you have	έχετε you have
έχει he/she/it has	έχουν they have

The **PAST SIMPLE** tense (I did, you bought etc) has the following endings (but note that changes have to be made to the form of the verb which comes before these endings):

πλήρωσ-α	I paid
πλήρωσ-ες	you paid
πλήρωσ-ε	he/she paid
πληρώσ-αμε	we paid
πληρώσ-ατε	you paid
πληρώσ-ανε	they paid

GRAMMAR

The past tense of the two useful verbs 'to be' and 'to have' is:

ήμουν	I was	ήμασταν	we were
ήσουν	you were	ήσασταν	you were
ήταν	he/she/it was	ήταν	they were

I was here last year
ήμουν εδώ πέρσι

είχα	I had	είχαμε	we had
είχες	you had	είχατε	you had
είχε	he/she/it had	είχαν	they had

did you have a car?
είχατε ένα αυτοκίνητο;

Here is a list of some useful verbs with their past simple in the first person:

present	*past simple*
βλέπω (see)	είδα
βρίσκω (find)	βρήκα
δίνω (give)	έδωσα
έρχομαι (come)	ήρθα
κάνω (do)	έκανα
λέω (say)	είπα
μένω (stay)	έμεινα
παίρνω (take)	πήρα
πηγαίνω (go)	πήγα
πίνω (drink)	ήπια
στέλνω (send)	έστειλα
τρώω (eat)	έφαγα

The simplest way of forming a *FUTURE TENSE* (the future continuous) in Greek is to take the present tense forms and add the word θα in front of them:

θα πληρώνω	I will be paying
θα πληρώνεις	you will ...
θα πληρώνει	he/she will ...
θα πληρώνουμε	we will ...
θα πληρώνετε	you will ...
θα πληρώνουν	they will ...

when will it be ready?
πότε θα είναι έτοιμο;

NEGATIVES are formed by putting the word δεν in front of the verb:

I don't speak Greek
δεν μιλώ Ελληνικά

CONVERSION TABLES

metres
1 metre = 39.37 inches or 1.09 yards

kilometres
1 kilometre = 0.62 or approximately ⅝ mile

to convert kilometres to miles: divide by 8 and multiply by 5

kilometres:	2	3	4	5	10	100
miles:	1.25	1.9	2.5	3.1	6.25	62.5

miles
to convert miles to kilometres: divide by 5 and multiply by 8

miles:	1	3	5	10	20	100
kilometres:	1.6	4.8	8	16	32	160

kilos
1 kilo = 2.2 or approximately 1⅕ pounds

to convert kilos to pounds: divide by 5 and multiply by 11

kilos:	4	5	10	20	30	40
pounds:	8.8	11	22	44	66	88

pounds
1 pound = 0.45 or approximately 5/11 kilo

litres
1 litre = approximately 1¾ pints or 0.22 gallons

Celsius
to convert to Fahrenheit: divide by 5, multiply by 9, add 32

Celsius:	10	15	20	25	28	30	34
Fahrenheit:	50	59	68	77	82	86	93

Fahrenheit
to convert Fahrenheit to Celsius: subtract 32, multiply by 5, divide by 9